The Feast

Mary (Lush) Hobson was born in London in 1926. She studied piano at the Royal Academy, raised four children and cared for a severely disabled husband before the first of her novels was published by Heinemann in 1980. In 1988 she started a Russian degree in London, studying in Moscow as the USSR collapsed. She developed a great affinity for Pushkin and still translates his work daily.

Mary's son Matthew, like Pushkin, died at thirty-eight. He is the subject of the poems *Death and the Biker*, republished with *The Feast*.

Also by Mary Hobson

Fiction
This Place is a Madhouse (1980)
Oh, Lily (1981)
Poor Tom (1983)
Promenade (2015)

Poetry
Death and the Biker (2009)

Translations
Aleksandr Griboedov's 'Woe from Wit': a commentary and translation (2005)
Evgenii Onegin, Pushkin, a parallel text (Moscow, 2011)
Evgenii Onegin, Pushkin; audio book (Naxos, London, 2012)

Forthcoming
Evgenii Onegin, Pushkin
After Onegin:
The Last Seven Years
in the Poems and Letters of Aleksandr Sergeevich Pushkin

The Feast
An Autobiography

Mary Hobson

Blessed is he who makes his bow
And leaves life's feast, with words unsaid,
His glass half-full, life's tale half-read,
Who suddenly discovers how
To part with it, as I know how
To part with my Onegin now.

The last words of Pushkin's novel in verse, *Evgenii Onegin*

Thorpewood Publishing
2015

First published in 2015
by Thorpewood Publishing
57 Thorpewood Avenue,
London SE26 4BY
thorpewoodpublishing@gmail.com

Author photograph
© matthewmarschner.com

Portrait of author featured on front cover
and in photograph © Eleanor Cantons

ISBN   978-1-910873-02-1 (hardback)
           978-1-910873-03-8 (paperback)
           978-1-910873-04-5 (eBook)

Printed in the UK and USA
by Lightning Source

Contents

Author's note

I want to express my gratitude to Sally Reed for her generosity in offering to type the manuscript of this book, and my admiration for her skill in deciphering it. I would like to thank my good, good friend Helen Shreeve. She has given me her time, her expertise and her encouragement. She has kept me going through the difficult bits every inch of the way in writing this autobiography and in getting it published. Most of all I thank her for knowing how much I wanted to write it. I want to thank my children for their loving, unfailing support. And Pushkin for writing his way into my heart with his poems and his letters like an old friend I never met.

Mary Hobson

For Neil, Matthew, Emma, Sarah, Lucy, Robert, Holly, Oliver, Alissandria, Eleanor, William, Rebecca and Tom

I

My father, Ernest, was the son of a country parson, one of eight children, four boys and four girls. The parson, the lowest of low church and a Hebrew scholar, used his religion to frighten his children into obedience; when this failed he beat them. On Sundays the curtains were drawn and laughter prohibited. 'Think what Jesus suffered, my boy.' Six year old Ernest, hiding on the window seat behind the drawn curtains, absorbed the terrible images in the only book allowed on this penitential day of rest – 'Fox's Book of Martyrs.' His mother, either preparing for or recovering from another pregnancy, lay down in a darkened room, and the children were brought up by Emma the housemaid.

At seven he was sent to a school for the sons of clergymen in which he was the only boarder. When the other boys went home his isolation was complete. Supper was brought to his room on a tray, and again he read the only available book – 'Ivanhoe'. Again and again. He could quote whole passages from memory. Later his studies in chemistry at Selwyn College, Cambridge, earned him a BA and an MA. Later still he became an Associate of the Institute of Chemistry and a Fellow of the Chemical Society. He had written his doctoral thesis but refused to pay the fee involved. However, he subsequently published a book entitled 'Oils, Fats and Waxes'. I suspect that this was it. It sounds like a thesis to me.

In 1914, at 26, he enlisted in the army as a private and served throughout the war without even the benefit of a 'blighty one' – an injury severe enough to merit a temporary reprieve in a British hospital. He rose to the rank of captain over the numerous bodies of those less fortunate and was discharged at the end of it all with the words 'Impatient of discipline'. He did claim one distinction though. When months in the trenches began to dim the men's enthusiasm he was sent to deliver what was known as 'Lush's blood lecture'. It contained vivid descriptions of Germans bayoneting their pregnant sisters and was, apparently, effective. Worthy of Fox himself. I only knew this, of course, because he used to tell us about it; true or not, it was what he wanted his family to believe.

My mother Adelaide was the illegitimate child – the term then in use – of a man wealthy enough to keep his mistress in some style in an apartment in Jermyn Street. Their daughter, surely a mistake, was spoiled for four years and then sent to a convent in Brussels, my grandmother being partly Irish and a Catholic. There she remained until the outbreak of war, when she returned to Jermyn Street, at 20, speaking only French, and having acquired three saints' names at her first communion – Hilda Winifred Millicent. My father always called her Millie. She called him Ern. She used to tell us that she had studied music at the Brussels Conservatoire; that on her return to London she learned shorthand and typing at a Pitman's School and ran her own export business, after working for a while in the law-courts. Somehow I grew up doubting this. All of it. In spite of the fact that her French was beautiful, she had clearly mastered shorthand and typing, could play anything put in front of her, had no idea how to cook and ran a small export business in her fifties. I still play from her copy of the Mozart sonatas, inscribed 'Adelaide Bradley. From Mother, Xmas 1907.' Posted to her in Brussels, presumably. She would have been 13.

Only since the internet made research into family history so much easier did I discover that she had almost certainly been telling the truth. I began to remember things. Being taken to have tea with my grandmother in Lyons tea shop, a rare event which I knew not to mention at home. Although my father supported her in her old age and rented her a room somewhere in Wimbledon, I never went there, and she never came to visit us. Never. This was, I understood, something to do with my father. The different surnames of her parents on my mother's birth certificate must have come as something of a shock to him when he obtained it at Somerset House prior to their marriage. I suspect that his biblical sense of justice would not allow him to visit the sins of the mother on her daughter; but he would not have That Woman in his home. I note that my cautious grandfather only recorded the first half of his double-barrelled name on this certificate. Even now that causes me a twinge of doubt. My mother's story does sound so much like a comforting defence against reality.

I was born of this unlikely union in 1926, the year of the general strike, in which my father drove a bus. Or so he told us. That I never doubted; although he never drove anything else. Fortunately I was too young to be ashamed. I was not their first child. My sister Daphne Millicent had been born four years earlier and was adored by her father. My mother wanted a boy. And four years after I was born Robert arrived. 'I tricked him' she used to tell me, proudly. 'He wouldn't have had any more. Said we couldn't afford it'. Robert was adored by my mother. I adored him too. It seemed the safest position. Although this precocious calculation did not prove to be entirely reliable.

My father, who should clearly have accepted the readership at Cambridge when it was offered to him, was ill-adapted to a life of research in the chemical industry. He could have lived happily ever after with his books and his laboratory in Cambridge. I would not then have been born, of course; not have been sitting here at eighty-seven, having fun. Ah, my poor father. I once asked him 'Which of all the jobs you had did you like the best?' He said, with rare feeling 'I hated them all.' But those first years of his marriage, in the house in Wimbledon Park, were a successful time for him. His wife had her black and gold drawing-room with the shining black upright piano, the black monkey-skin rug, the cake-stand in black lacquer, inlaid with mother of pearl, the black and gold wall-paper. Upstairs there was a nanny in our yellow nursery with the black and white frieze of children bowling hoops in silhouette. It had a rocking horse. And downstairs there was Miss Biddy, who did everything. I see my mother in black velvet, cloche hat and waist-length pearls, telling the large sweating woman in a cap and apron, bent over the wash-board – it must have been Monday – 'Keep an eye on her.' She left to drink coffee with friends; I sat in my high-chair and worried. I didn't mind her keeping me. But I watched her take the flat iron from the stove, watched her spit on it, heard the hiss, saw the steam, and hoped most fervently that she would not iron me.

Ah, my elegant mother, who had not yet lost faith in her husband's ability to keep her in the manner to which she was accustomed.

Three more things come to mind when I recall that house. Two remained in my memory, one was told to me later and more than once by my father. He used to laugh about the evening when, exasperated by my constant crying, he came up to the nursery, held my nose with one hand and put the other over my mouth. Thereby achieving a blessed silence. I have, of course, no recollection of the event. What I do remember is my reluctant reconciliation with my father, at the age of four. This took place about two months after Robert was born. My father brought home presents for Daphne and me. Harrods money-boxes. Solid, silver, squat round ones, with special slots for each kind of coin, and a vertical slit so that you could see the pile mounting. There was even a small hole in the top into which you could insert a rolled-up note – in the unlikely event of your being given one. They were prepared for every eventuality at Harrods. Who can forget the resourceful cleft sticks offered to the hero of Waugh's blissful 'Scoop'? Surely a tribute to this very quality. My Mother took me up in her arms. 'Say thank you to Daddy' she pleaded. 'Thank you' I said. Grudgingly. Under pressure. It was the first time that I had spoken to him.

The other thing I remember concerned my sister. Daphne, eight years old with a controlling imagination, summoned me from the nursery. I must wear something yellow and carry something yellow. Otherwise. The unspoken threat left every terrible option open. There were yellow flowers on my dress, so I took a yellow crayon from the box and followed her into her room. On the semi-circular shelf which filled the miniature bay-window stood something tall and jagged, concealed beneath a sheet. It was the secret of all magic, she told me. For a breathless moment I believed. Then doubt overcame me. I tore off the sheet to reveal the pile of books and toys. One or two clattered to the floor. I have had trouble with believing ever since.

Ah, and a fourth thing. I dreamed that I came downstairs and there were large cream coloured, upturned metal claws sticking out of the wall, somewhere between a beseeching hand and an agricultural implement. I ran into the kitchen where Daphne and my parents were sitting round the table. But as I tried to tell them they turned to greenish metal. I told them when I woke up though. I took them to show them. When the claws weren't there I still insisted that I had seen them.

Then one day there were packing-cases everywhere; the curtains were taken down and the windows whitewashed. Miss Biddy had gone. So had nanny. We were leaving the house in Wimbledon Park. Because the door-handles squeaked, or so my mother told me. At four it seemed an adequate explanation.

II

The house in Sidcup, one of a raw new development, was a disappointment to everyone but me. I'm sure Robert would have been disappointed, but at a few months old he was not of an age to protest. Daphne was angry because she had to share a room with me; my mother concealed her sense of betrayal with difficulty; my father really suffered. He had trusted a partner in a chemical enterprise and was perhaps the only person to feel surprise when the man decamped with the money he had invested. It was 1930. He had to find work, fast. He named the house 'Montauban' and set out to find some. Our mother made us kneel with her in the tiny drawing room, shorn of everything she had valued except the shining black piano, and pray that Daddy would get a job. She wrote the name my father had chosen on a strip of paper and pinned it to the front gate; but the milkman said it made his wounds ache, so she removed it. One day, when I have time, I will look into that name. But I am sure that I shall find it to be the site of a terrible defeat in the war to end all wars. That is how my father looked. Defeated. We had what seemed to me, at four, a huge garden. But we were not allowed to play with the children next door – 'He' was a bus driver. My father creosoted quantities of lathes and built a trellis which he attached to the top of the fence, so that no one could see his shame; but it blew down in the first strong wind. My mother laughed. She was not a sensitive woman, nor was she very intelligent. But she had that quality called 'nous'. A sort of brutal assurance. I think it was one of the reasons I irritated her so much, with my nightmares and my terror of the dark.

At six began the happiest period of my childhood. I went to school. The Manor House, it was called. An old red-brick building, left over from another age. Daphne and I cycled there and back every day; meeting a car in Sidcup then was a rare event. The classroom I remember had dark red flock wallpaper. There we were given exercise books ruled with faint blue lines, at least an inch and a quarter apart; above and below these lines were other, fainter ones for letters which stuck up or hung down. I can hardly describe the shock of delight on discovering that the shapes we attempted to copy between them made sounds. And that two or three or four of them together made words. Actual words that I knew. When we had mastered these fat letters and progressed to fitting them between ever narrower lines, there was even a picture-book with the words 'Ruth, can you see Rover? Rover can see Ruth.' But best of all was the book with no pictures. Then you were set free into a world of print. A parallel world where real people lived.

It took Millie about three years to engineer our return to Wimbledon. Ern found the first of all those many jobs he hated, possibly through the power of prayer, possibly in self-defence – my mother was not one to let matters lie. And in 1934, or thereabouts, we moved into the house in Vineyard Hill Road.

My father and I took refuge in reading. There were no books or book-shelves at home, but there was the Wimbledon Public Library. He always chose cowboy or detective stories; I was not discriminating. I would read anything. Dickens, Georgette Heyer, Walter Scott, fourpenny school-girls. I should explain that these last were a series of cheap paper-back books with black and yellow covers, set in girls' boarding schools. They misinformed me about larks in the dorm and cricket matches, descriptions of which always started with the sentence: 'The day of the match dawned fine and clear.' There we would have sat, the pair of us, evening after evening, scorching our shins around the gas-fire in the lounge; but Millie was not a reader. She expected to be entertained with conversation. 'What am I going to do?' she would ask, angrily, if she saw my fingers straying to the book stuffed down the side of the sofa. I was still reading Robert's bed-time story at that stage, but he soon joined us.

Daphne was different. We attended a school together called 'The Study', where she made friends. Robert and I were ginger and freckled; she was mousey, sallow-skinned and very, very thin, apparently as the result of whooping-cough contracted in the year I was born. She and I quarrelled constantly. Robert and I were inseparable. I was nearly ten when Millie decided that I had asthma and needed to live by the sea; she set about finding a boarding school for me. I knew that I didn't have asthma, but she explained that it was our secret way of getting me this great opportunity. The fourpenny school-girls enabled me to share her view of the matter; I could hardly wait for September.

Looking back, I can sympathise. I had added frequent attacks of what were known as 'Mary's hysterics' to the nightmares and fear of the dark. The cause of them was unknown, to me or anyone else. But I can remember lying on the floor, screaming and sobbing uncontrollably. Boarding school must have seemed to her a restful alternative. And then my father's behaviour was becoming noticeably stranger. One incident. No more, I promise. Just so that you get the picture. Daphne and I were in the garden with him. It was a fine summer's day. He made us stand back to back, arms outstretched as if crucified; then he used our skipping ropes to tie a broom handle between them, laughing in an unpleasant high-pitched manner, saying 'now see if you can get out of that.' This was too much even for my mother. She came out and put a stop to it. I can't help feeling that some of her reasons for this asthma deception were excellent; even if she did want Robert for herself.

Autumn was approaching. My father read the clothing list in horror; my mother took me to Daniel Neals. I remember the trunk, light brown with my initials on it in black. M.E.L. Mary Elizabeth Lush. The uniform for morning, the uniform to change into at tea-time, the uniform for weekends, the hacking-jacket, jodhpurs and bowler for riding; I could go on. But won't. I had never seen such an excess of new stuff. It cost One Hundred Pounds. Friends were invited to view it; my mother's friends, of course. A hundred pounds was a truly enormous sum in 1936; a 'thousand-a-year man' was considered to be doing well in my parents' small circle. My father had yet to achieve that status. God knows how he paid for it all. But it nailed me in place, that trunkful. My mother had given me this wonderful present; how could I possibly tell her that the boarding school she had chosen for me was less than perfect?

III

D isillusion was swift. It took about twenty-four hours. But I boarded the school train at Victoria in a state of delirious pride and travelled hopefully to the great opportunity. My deficiencies were all exposed by the end of the first supper. I was wearing the wrong blouse, I ate with my mouth open – I had not been aware of this and am still proud of the speed with which I lied that I had asthma and couldn't help it. 'Look at the newbug' they cried in delight; there is always a natural victim, and I was it. However, I hadn't quite given up.

The space above the new gymnasium had been partitioned with varnished pine into numerous cubicles for two; two iron bedsteads, separated by a small chest-of-drawers and a curtain at the entrance. Prefects slept in the only two single cubes at the far corners. I was to share one of these double cubes with another new girl called Sheila. Surely she would be my Best Friend? When she stopped crying. I realised my mistake long before that; she managed to make her feelings clear between sobs.

I have written about the bullying in this school in a novel; but there I was free to invent a resistance movement for my misfit. My own plan was less courageous. I retreated into my head and thought up avoidance tactics. It was a good position from which to observe things but it didn't invite friendship. I didn't mind. They were all horrible anyway. Much worse than Daphne. All I needed was a safe place to read in those dangerous, unsupervised moments. You were alright with a grown-up. Lessons were a refuge, and so was the hour and twenty minutes of prep after tea. Scratching away with my relief nib, dipped in the desk-top inkwell filled by the ink monitor; a blissful silence only broken by the sighs of those children who could have managed quite well without lessons. I have to admit that the splendid marks I achieved as a result of my diligence only served to alienate the others still further. It just wasn't natural. 'Her father beats her if she doesn't swat' they told each other. There had to be a reason.

The bullying took the form that it usually takes in a small group of ten-year-olds. A leader emerges and the rest join in to avoid being bullied themselves. Moral courage is not well-developed in children of ten. A small girl called Molly was thrown into a bed of nettles. I'm glad to be able to tell you that I was hiding in the lavatories at the time. Simple physical violence of that sort was rare; methods were usually more subtle. The one that is giving me gooseflesh as I recall it involved the blackboard. It was soon discovered that squeaking the chalk or scraping fingernails on it reduced me to a kind of mindless frenzy. It was irresistible. One child did the squeaking, the rest held me down. I don't think the whiteboard can offer the same opportunities. At least I hope not.

The abdication came and went during that first term; it was nearly Christmas, so we sang 'Hark the herald angels sing, Mrs Simpson stole our king' and forgot about it. I sat in the various safe places I'd found, including the boot room, a short dash across some cobbles, and dreamed up another fantasy: Going home for the holidays. I had already counted the days; now I drove up Vineyard Hill Road in a car – it must have been a taxi, we didn't have a car – waving my lacrosse stick from the window. Neighbours lined the streets and cheered; the milkman (the handsome one) shouted 'She's home!' The day came. I went home. It did not happen like this. I bored them all with invented school stories, they talked about things that they'd done when I wasn't there.

For the next two years I continued to travel between Wimbledon and Worthing. I remember a period during one holiday which the grownups referred to as The Crisis. We all moved, briefly, to Dorset, where one of my father's brothers ran a small boarding school for boys. I even attended a local day school when term started. Only for one morning though. I came back at lunch time and refused to go there ever again; television had not yet ironed out regional accents and I hadn't understood a single word all morning. On the 30th of September 1938, Neville Chamberlain returned from Munich and declared that he had achieved 'peace in our time'. This appeared to be a good thing to everyone except my father, who was furious and said he was ashamed to be British.

My mother had been making plans again. My school reports had convinced her that I was clever and must attend St. Pauls School for Girls. She had either anticipated Chamberlain's declaration by almost a month, or she'd had enough of my father's sister-in-law. One way or another Wimbledon was said to be safe again and I started at my new school. This escape from boarding school was nothing short of miraculous, but with the best will in the world - which, in the circumstances, I had – I could make nothing of it.

I travelled to Brook Green every morning by underground, changing at Earls Court. The journey was just long enough to eat a tube of Smarties if you sucked them instead of crunching them. At twelve it seemed quite an adventure. But the school itself was baffling. St. Pauls was enormous, or seemed so to me. The teachers were all called 'Ma'am', which rendered them unmemorable; I never learned their names. I was frequently found wandering by a kindly senior, having been sent to Miss Somebody's classroom. I arrived late for a lot of lessons and never quite found out what was going on. I could see that it was a wonderful school; the music department was overpowering. The shade of Gustav Holst still hung over it – people played concertos with the orchestra at the end-of-term concert. Herbert Howells, who had succeeded Holst, once asked me to turn a page over for him when he nodded. There can only have been one turn; my two years of gentle piano lessons with the elderly Miss Green had not equipped me for anything more serious. However, he nodded, I turned, and fell passionately in love with him. Falling in love with music teachers, regardless of their gender, was to become a habit which only leaving school could dislodge.

Apart from Herbert Howells, one other incident comes to mind. Millie loved a bargain. She had bought two pairs of shoes from a friend which were my size. White with either navy or brown heels and toes. They had little lavatory heels and the edges of the coloured bits were punched like brogues. Now, I would love them. Pure 30s, my favourite thing. Even then I went to school in them, only slightly apprehensive. Heels were against the rules, I was told by a shocked teacher – the uniform code was rigid. But Millie was not willing to abandon her bargain. She took them to a cobbler and asked him to cut an inch off the heels. He protested, but he did it, and I staggered to school for a day or two in them before she would admit defeat.

The summer of '39 was spent, as all our summer holidays were spent, in a hotel in Worthing; later I wondered if that was really where she spent her childhood, as opposed to the convent in Brussels. This year was special. My father went home at the end of our stay to his work as an industrial research chemist; Daphne went with him; at seventeen, she now had a job in a bank. But my mother, Bob and I moved to a boarding house called 'Dinard'; we seemed to be waiting for something to happen. And on the 3rd of September it did. We sat in the front room with our landlady and listened in silence to the wireless. We heard Chamberlain's voice, weary and resigned: '...I have to tell you that no such undertaking has been received and that consequently this country is at war with Germany.' Our landlady, whose husband had been killed in the last war with Germany, began to sob hysterically. Robert and I, experiencing a rare intrusion into the adult world, looked on in amazement, until my mother took charge and sent us to our room. Within minutes the import of this new state of affairs was underlined by a first, false-alarm air-raid siren. If shelters had already been built I don't recall being taken to one. I suspect that the continuous note of the 'all-clear' had sounded before anyone in Dinard had decided how they should react to the original wailing threat.

After that nothing seemed to happen. Except the worst thing. My mother and Robert returned to Wimbledon; I went back to my old boarding school where, it was reasonably argued, I would be safer.

The war soon became real enough. The blitz began – though I only experienced the worst of it during the holidays. Robert would walk to his school between air-raids; the boys gathered in the shelters, collected work to be done at home, and waited for the 'all-clear' before hurrying back. He developed a nervous tic in one eye. My mother took him out of school and the four of them went for a holiday together in Herne Bay. It was a really good plan. The tic disappeared. But the holiday in Herne Bay became something they talked about and I envied.

Then in 1941 my school was evacuated to a hotel in Cornwall. Porthledden, St. Just, is one of the bleakest spots on God's earth. The hotel stood on a hill overlooking Cape Cornwall, which jutted out into the Atlantic; the chimney of a disused tin-mine marked its summit. On a clear day you could see the Scilly Isles, but I don't remember many clear days. You could lean on the wind. We were all to meet in London and travel by train, a journey of ten hours, to our new home, teachers and children, at a time when the family had just moved to Liverpool, following the next job in my father's succession of jobs. My mother hated Liverpool as much as she had hated Sidcup, and for the same reason; neither of them was Wimbledon. For her I am sure that even one night in London was better than nothing. We travelled together and spent that night at the Regent Palace Hotel in Piccadilly, where she told me she had met my father. Still in his uniform looking, she managed to imply, deceptively handsome. There was inevitably, an air-raid. Everyone spent the night in the basement grill-room, sleeping on chairs, tables, on the floor, in dressing gowns, being drawn by war-artist Topolski. If you ever happen to spot a plain 14 year-old who would pass for ten in one of his vivid drawings that was me.

The sleeping arrangements at our temporary school presented an additional hazard; the place couldn't accommodate all the children. Some of us slept in the three small cottages at the end of the drive known as Upper Praze, Middle Praise and Lower Prase. (I never saw the names written down, so I'm offering a choice of spellings; I favour the first one. It emphasises the alien qualities of Cornwall as a foreign country). One member of staff slept in each cottage, but not, of course, from eight o'clock at night. This opened up a dangerously unsupervised period without the benefit of a single refuge. I did run out into the night in my pyjamas once, but only once; at the risk of offending the Tourist Board, no one in their right mind would go outside on a winter night in Cornwall. A wrecker perhaps. However we only stayed there for a year. No bombs fell on Worthing, and in the following September we moved back to a school whose familiarity seemed almost welcoming.

Millie, meanwhile, had found a flat in Wimbledon. She left Ern renting a room in a house owned by two old ladies and moved the rest of us back to London. I was never really sure if he noticed we'd left. He must have enjoyed evening after evening reading his cowboy stories; but eventually he joined us. It may only have been a brief interval while he looked for a job in London; but I suspect that Millie, as usual, had simply taken matters into her own hands.

I was only there during the holidays, of course. But I remember the bombing, the reassuring sound of the ack-ack defending us, and was at first protected by the certainty that it couldn't happen to me; that went, suddenly, when I saw quite plainly that it could. After that I was sure that it would. At the first wail of an air-raid siren I could feel myself buried under tons of rubble. There were bombs dropped on Wimbledon; one fell on Wimbledon Hill. The blast must have weakened the grip of our ceilings – a day or two later the one in the lounge collapsed onto the carpet. The way Millie told it, she had been lying on the sofa with a headache and had just got up to make herself a cup of tea. The two bedroom ceilings on either side of the lounge seemed unaffected, but Millie had more faith in the front bedroom, so we all slept together there on mattresses. And I remember a land-mine in Worthing, probably dropped by someone who couldn't find where he'd meant to drop it. It was close enough to shatter the window-glass. I was a prefect by then, sleeping in a single cube; I was under that iron bed-stead with the lumpy striped mattress on top of me before the last of it tinkled to the ground. A heartening example of the instinct for self-preservation.

When the school returned to Worthing, a wonderful thing happened. It had acquired a real piano teacher. Someone genuinely interested in what she was doing. Joan Last, she was called; though not, of course, by me. Miss Last would eventually teach at the Royal Academy of Music. Indeed, I could never quite understand what she was doing in that school. I fell in love with her too. And with music. But the first summer back in Worthing was devoted to passing the School Certificate, later to be replaced by O Levels and then by GCSE. I was embarrassed by the results; even I could see that I hadn't needed to work that hard. I had obtained Matriculation Exemption, which would have been the next stage; after that came Higher School Certificate, the prelude to a university education. But the school did not teach to that level. I 'added' Latin, which I loved, and then, at 16, threw myself into practising.

Here was the very thing I needed; a productive refuge from the difficult business of talking to people. By taking one of those Associated Board exams every term I arrived at a teacher's L.R.A.M. at 19 in a state of terror, just as the war came to an end. Everyone celebrated, except my father, who was disgusted by the election of a labour government under Clement Attlee to see to the peace; I practised scales in double octaves.

I have one very clear memory of that examination. I sat down to play the first piece, the Bach prelude and fugue in C sharp major Book I from the 48. That prelude was fatal. It involved a rapid rotatory movement of the right hand indistinguishable from shaking with fear. I was halfway down the first page before they could stop me. 'Do you usually play it at that speed?' one of the examiners asked. I shook my head; speech was out of the question. They were so kind, that board. I probably shouldn't have passed, but they apparently took to the Brahms, and let me through.

I was now qualified, musically at least, to join the real world. But it took another two years. The qualification seemed to justify my paralysis; I began to teach. I saw at once that I would never make a piano teacher. I could not let anything pass. My pupils gave up, which I couldn't help feeling was a good thing; they all seemed tone-deaf and totally uninterested. I hope I didn't destroy a real talent; but I suspect their parents had ordered music lessons with extra milk and Radio Malt after breakfast. (A form of sweet, sticky tooth-rot then very popular with the middle classes; it was said to promote a child's health in some way).

I might have stayed there until I turned into Miss Green, instilling a lifelong dislike of music in my pupils, if another young teacher had not joined the staff. She told me that the LCC gave grants to people who wanted to study. This was an entirely new idea to me. Another three or four years at the Royal Academy of Music would postpone all other decisions. It seemed that I would need a second study. A violin teacher was found for me who lent me a violin and I started work. What a marvellous instrument. Unlike the piano it had ways of getting from one note to another. It required no spatial awareness whatsoever; just a good ear, which I have. Judging distances, finding places is a gift I do not possess, on the piano keyboard or, indeed, anywhere else. I have no navigational skills. Miss Green hadn't noticed that I had to memorise everything before I could play it. By the time Joan Last took a hand it was too late. Not even she could teach me to look at the music and magically guess where the keys were. I practised Sevcik's Lagenwechsel assiduously and — at the risk of repeating myself — fell in love with my violin teacher (again, female). I applied for and received a grant. And on my 21st birthday I finally left school.

I would like to leave Chapter 3 on this happy note, but I've promised myself to be absolutely honest, so I have to report that my purse, containing all my money and my ticket to London, was stolen in the ladies' room on Brighton Station. I managed to explain this to the stationmaster, who gave me another ticket and enough money to travel from Victoria to Wimbledon, to be repaid later. It only occurs to me now that he probably took me for a rather slow fifteen-year-old, and what were my parents thinking of?

IV

The first year at the Royal Academy of Music was wonderful. No other word for it. Solitude was not only justified but essential. Of course, other students formed quintets, fell in and out of love, went to parties, as a ground-bass to their studies; I practised; six, seven, eight hours a day. The neighbours in our small block of flats, reasonably, complained. Millie found a hay-loft in a Wimbledon mews occupied by milk-horses. My spectacular 21st birthday present had been a Broadwood semi-grand, then already 45 years old. It was Joan Last who suggested it. An elderly friend was moving into a small flat and was willing to sell it very cheaply to someone who would love it and play it. It was one of Millie's bargains. She offered to pay the £70 in instalments, and my last months of studying with Miss Last were over-shadowed by her failure to do so regularly. I can only hope the poor woman got her money eventually. It's too late to tell her that I have loved and played it ever since. It now has keys like a mouthful of loose teeth, but it has retained its gentle tone.

So – the piano was manoeuvred through the hay door from the roof of a removal van and I was free to practise without disturbing anyone. Well, the milk-horses used to shift about a bit when I really got going. It was stifling in summer and freezing in winter but I loved it.

The three year performers' course for which I had enrolled offered bronze, silver and gold medals at the end of each year. Claude Pollard, my teacher, entered me for the silver medal. I played the Cesar Franck Prelude, Chorale and Fugue, a performance in an empty Duke's Hall to a board of professors sitting, it seemed to me, a mile or so away. The practising had paid off. (It often does). My heart was thumping, my hands felt like bunches of cold bananas, but I was awarded both the silver medal and that year's Townsend Scholarship. I didn't know there was a Townsend Scholarship and that all the 'silver' candidates had been competing for it, until someone congratulated me in Baker Street. I hugged the dream of becoming a pianist and went back to the hay-loft; I nurtured it in spite of a disabling stage-fright which, while I was still at school, had resulted in an 'out-of-body' experience. It was during a one-handed performance of Chopin's Fantaisie Impromptu at the Brighton Festival. Both hands were required, but one hand or the other kept losing the thread. I was up in the ornate ceiling of the Chinese room at the Pavilion, looking down on myself and thinking 'why don't you just get up and walk off?' I feel for Joan Last. If she had one flaw, it was her irritation with my unpredictable performances. I could play it to her; why not to a bored adjudicator and a roomful of competitors, all playing the same set-piece, all hell-bent on winning? Perhaps she shared Millie's view. 'Don't take any notice of them. They're cabbages. Just rows of cabbages.' Millie didn't think much of other people. If she had known the person who said 'Hell is other people' I am sure she would have got on very well with him. I have the impression that, apart from Robert, whom she adored still, she despised everyone, my father in particular. Now, living with the family, I began to observe them all. Millie made her disdain for her husband quite plain; Ern, with his greater intelligence, lured her into bullying him in front of her friends until they became acutely embarrassed and hated her for it.

Robert got the expected brilliant results in his School Certificate, obtaining Matriculation Exemption, then disappointed my father's last hope of a child at university (music didn't count) by deciding to be a stage designer and taking a job painting scenery. I was still very close to Robert and became, more by association than any endeavour on my part, close to his great friend, the novelist-to-be, David Hughes. Don't misunderstand me. I loved him. He was so intelligent and so handsome; he once wrote me a poem in white ink on black paper, tied with white ribbon. But I cannot claim to have been his 'girl-friend'. This was not something I knew how to do. It was fun, though. David, Robert and I formed the Failures Club. Failure seemed so much more sophisticated than success. Easier, too. They were only eighteen but I had no such excuse. This delightful interlude was cut short, however, by National Service. The two of them went off to spend 18 months in the R.A.F. When I said goodbye to David on Wimbledon station

I could have wept for his long dark wavy hair, now shaved into a regulation short back and sides.

Daphne was already married with her first child, a daughter called Mary. She was much nicer than me. Fatally unselfish. If you like me, you would have loved Daphne. Or Vicky, as we had been instructed to call her, since her affair with one of our talented conscientious objectors in Liverpool; an actor who told her that she looked much more like a Vicky, and gave her a china powder-box with a portrait of the young Queen Victoria on the lid. Have I told you about the conscientious objectors in Liverpool? I find that I haven't – and they are worth a brief digression. A group of them was billeted in the empty house opposite our own. The German bombers were going for the docks in the winter of 1941 and they acted as firefighters. There was no hot water in their billet and the patriotic ladies of Liverpool refused to offer them baths. Millie didn't mind. 'They can bath here,' she told the unhappy sergeant in charge of them. So five or six of them gathered round the fire for tea and whatever Millie had managed to scrounge in that time of strict rationing. What a talented bunch. Only a war could have brought them to our fireside. Christopher Fry, Michael Gough… I wish I could remember all their names. Michael told such stories about his Irish uncle who demanded that his servants take him to the Spanish civil war, and chased them round the estate in his wheelchair, threatening them with a rifle, when they very sensibly refused. My father wasn't used to laughter, but Michael could make him remove his pince-nez and mop up the tears.

But I was telling you about my sister. When she was four, Daphne was taken to Hamley's toy shop and told that she could choose. Anything. Probably to compensate for my arrival. She havered for a while between a bear and a beautifully dressed china doll, then chose the bear and cried all the way home. It finally emerged that she had wanted the doll but the bear looked so sad. I remembered this family legend when she broke off her engagement to a charming Czech doctor to marry Jack, a man with many problems.

At some point in the four years I eventually spent at the RAM, I played three concertos at the orchestral rehearsals conducted by

Clarence Raybould. The first, Mozart in D minor, could only leave me with a sense of dissatisfaction; for Mozart, nothing but perfection will do. But how lucky I am to have had those three opportunities. The second was by Glazunov: it has a conventional first movement which rises to a near-unbearable pitch of romantic despair then goes off into a theme and variations. Not great music. But the exhilaration of reaching that climax, you and the orchestra, building it up slowly, holding back and then letting it rip, not thinking about anything... While you're recovering from this sexual imagery, let me tell you about the third concerto. Now that is great music. Brahms' 1st in D minor. I love it even more than the 2nd. I only played the first movement of it. But there is a moment in that first movement where a French horn comes in with two notes which usually express finality – soh-doh, in an upward direction. Here they don't. There's a pause. It tries again, manages one note higher, gives up and plays the first two again – twice; then, using that higher note as a lever, it soars up an octave to one of triumphant uncertainty. The piano answers with three slow descending chords and together we set out to explore the world... Oh hell. It's beautiful. Shall I hum it? Do put it on your iPod.

One of the equally memorable but less satisfying aspects of my years at the RAM was Millie's attempt to 'bring me out of myself'. I think she began to realise that, at twenty-one, my behaviour lacked something. I was invited to the 21st birthday party of her bridge-playing friend's daughter and stood throughout the evening with a glass of gin and something in my hand, failing to utter a single word. The friend phoned Millie next morning. 'Is Mary a bit.... simple?' she asked. That did it. Millie laughed as she told me but evidently took it seriously. I was sent, during that first long summer vacation, to spend six weeks with a French family. I'm sure the French are lovely really; but I'm left with a damaging minus to overcome when meeting any of them.

Her final effort, arranged through a golfing friend, involved three months in Verona. Now the Italians are lovely. If you can put together three words of their language they are prepared to help with the rest. I learned holiday Italian and fell helplessly in love with an Irishman twice my age. His wife was my age – 25 – but she was keeping cool up in the hills with their baby. I had never experienced (you may have noticed if you've read this far) anything like it. If I had been capable of sensible thought, instead of feeling faint when I saw someone in a crowd wearing what looked like his jacket, I expect I would have been shocked. But I was not capable of it. However. I had just time to discover to my amazement that sex was easy; all you needed was someone who knew how to do it. The next morning a telegram arrived: 'Return at once, mother seriously ill'. If it had been signed 'The Thought Police' instead of 'Father', the message could not have been clearer. I packed and left.

Millie's cancer developed slowly. She was not to be told of the diagnosis, Ern insisted; we were all to act normally. We agreed and entered upon a long period of the most destructive dishonesty. All hope of intimacy was lost – to my mother, to us all. But it was as much as my father could bear. For me, acting normally presented problems. I had been awarded the gold medal at the end of my second year – (Liapunov: 'Carillon from 12 Transcendental Studies') and had achieved nothing much since. At the end of four years I had left. I could see that some sort of decision was now required. In this I was assisted by a dream – I was lying in a black, shiny coffin with an interior of polished pinkish wood. Or a coffin-shaped Steinway. And I was lying in it the wrong way round, with my head at the narrow end. I could take a hint. It was time to abandon the dream.

At this point I heard on the wireless that the WVS (not yet Royal) needed women of 25 or more to run clubs for the troops overseas. The Korean War was then at its height. Absent-mindedly pursuing yet another dream, I saw myself handing out mugs of cocoa beneath a hail of bullets. I rang the telephone number they gave and went up to Tothill Street to fill in a form. It asked; 'Where would you prefer to serve? BAOR, MELF, or FARELF?' I had not the slightest idea what these initials meant. They were bound to think I was an idiot if I had to ask. Wouldn't they? I studied the acronyms. I quite liked the look of MELF. It started with my initials. Mary Elizabeth Lush. I went for MELF. Which was how, a month or two later, I found myself in Egypt.

V

After a brief stay in Cyprus, where my likely usefulness was assessed at the Famagusta Holiday Camp for soldiers on leave, I was posted to Geneifa. This was, in every sense, a dump; about half-way down the Suez Canal (I think) in the middle of a lot of sand, men were guarding sheds full of stuff. IO Base Ordinance Depot. But for the heat and the flies, it might have been Margate. I shared a double-skinned tent in its own compound with Frances, the only other woman; we ate in the officers' mess, where we were out of place and unwelcome. I sympathise, but where else could we eat?

This guarding apparently took all day, so the club which we were to run for the national-servicemen only opened for three or four hours in the evening. The NAAFI, where the brutal licentious got their char and wads (I'm just giving you a taste of the jargon in fashion in the mess) was next to our club. We played record requests, held snooker tournaments, sent flowers via Inter Flora for the homesick. Cocoa and bullets were not involved. It left us with a lot of spare time which we spent with the officers; fraternising with the 'other ranks' was strictly forbidden. I learned to sail a snipe on the Bitter Lakes with a Wing-Commander based in Ismailia and formed an unsatisfactory relationship with one of the officers from our mess – married, of course. The officers were quite as bored and frustrated as the national-servicemen, but less homesick. He used to tell me how much his wife irritated him when she bought chocolate biscuits they couldn't afford. But we dined at the French Club in Ismailia; once we swam in the Bitter Lakes by moonlight... It sounds romantic, but it was not. I had, by now, constructed an outside person who stood in for me and navigated her way through this lunacy while I hid inside. It seemed the best way.

On Fridays Frances and I took turns to visit North Camp, where the club was a huge tent surrounded by hundreds of smaller tents and even more sand. What they were all doing there I never discovered. But the lonely ones came in to talk, request records and play table-tennis on the sandy, uneven ground. A tough young Catholic called Brian offered to teach me; he showed me some mean shots. My favourite was the one in which the ball arrived on the other side of the net with a backward spin and a forward impetus which left it juddering on the table, quite failing to bounce. I've loved that game ever since; I still play it whenever I get the chance, which is not, of course, very often. I brought him a rosary made of olive stones from the Mount of Olives when I went on leave to Jerusalem. I had laid this rosary on the tomb of Christ; I was moved by his emotion when I gave it to him, and mystified, as I always am when confronted by faith.

The only dangerous thing I ever did in Egypt was to travel by jeep. Our army was not popular in the Canal Zone in 1952; we could only go outside the barbed wire that surrounded us in IO B.O.D if accompanied by a soldier with a sten-gun. He sat behind me with this gun and every time we lurched over a hump in the sandy track I hoped he had remembered the safety catch.

No. There was one really dangerous thing. I took two bus-loads of eighteen-year-old national servicemen on a picnic in some gulf whose name I have forgotten. It was my turn, and no one seemed to think it unwise. It was said that Norman Hartnell designed our uniforms; if he did, I am grateful to him. All that practising had worked off the fat. I was slim, and looked younger than my twenty-five years. More to the point, I was an actual woman. But that green buttoned overall with dark red detail kept me safe. The only dodgy moment occurred when I decided to swim and took it off. I did have a swimsuit under it. Nevertheless that has to rank as one of the most stupid things I ever did. I think I must have looked so horrified when the nicely-brought-up young man made his move that he apologised, and I got back into my Norman Hartnell.

Every now and then a lady from Tothill Street – 'Totters', she called it – would pay us a pastoral visit. She was not impressed with our efforts; she herself would spend whole evenings in the sergeants' bar. 'You should mingle with the chaps', she exhorted us. You could hear the shouting and the breaking glass 50 yards from that bar. One good mingle might well have finished us off; not even Norman Hartnell could have saved us. Why did I stay? Our air-fares were paid, of course, at the beginning and end of the eighteen months. We could only leave earlier at our own expense. So I stayed.

I remember the whole family meeting me at the airport on my return. For a split second I saw them all through the eyes of a stranger; then they were the people I knew. I tried hard to show them that I had changed, but of course I too lapsed almost instantly into my former self.

I had now to find some work. A friend of my sister's knew an antique dealer looking for an assistant and I went up to Old Brompton Road for an interview. I was to mind the shop while he drove all over the countryside looking for old ladies with undervalued antiques. I lasted three months. This was because, as I stood in the back of the shop on that first day, willing potential customers to walk past, a man from a ministry turned up. He wanted six and two arms. Regency. There was just such a set of chairs stored out of sight near the back. I showed it to him, then spent far too long trying to decode the price on the ticket. He was beginning to sigh. Finally I told him the outrageous sum. 'Right' he said. 'Have it delivered.' I just managed to stop myself from explaining that that was the starting price, now he was supposed to haggle. I took down the address and was amazed to find that I'd made my first sale. Not, however, as amazed as the dealer. Overjoyed would not be an exaggeration. It was a boring, late and not entirely original set of chairs that he was keen to get rid of, he told me. I sold very little else. But that first sale must have deluded him; he gave me one chance after another. I expect I would have been sacked sooner if he had been there to see me in action. I remember a young woman who came in to buy the Queen Anne desk in the window for her fiancé as a wedding present. Well. What would you have done? I told her not to. Neither the period nor the integrity of it were as advertised. I told her that too. My fakerloo, as he called himself and his colleagues when he was in his jocular mood, had added one or two new bits, then distressed them with a gimlet and some cigarette ash. His most ingenious trick was to conjure four chairs out of a much less saleable three, and play honest dealer; confessing that a leg here and there was not quite right. After all, every one of those four chairs had three good legs.

Losing that job was the greatest piece of good fortune. I am sure you will be glad to hear that it changed the entire course of my life. Bob – as Robert had become after five minutes in the RAF, despite all Millie's previous efforts – was now working as designer at Wolverhampton Rep. A firm manufacturing agricultural vehicles wished to display a tractor at the Windsor Agricultural Show against a back-drop of a Tudor Village. Bob had found another penniless designer to help him. But the pair of them had spent more time drinking than painting; they came to London to complete the work on site. The other young man had already migrated from Liverpool to Finchley Road, where he was sharing a flat with some Australians. They were both hungry and I was at home when Bob phoned. Would I make them some lunch? I cooked the two things I did best, Spaghetti Bolognese and lemon-meringue pie, and waited for them in a state of high anxiety verging on terror.

I can only attribute what happened next to the presence of Bob. We were as close as ever, and he was perhaps the only person with whom I was able to approach being myself. They arrived. I was introduced to Neil, Bob's drinking partner. We ate and talked and I even said one or two things that made them laugh. Millie was then running her tiny export business – phrases come back to me, like Guest, Keen and Nettlefold, pro-forma invoice – so we sat there, just the three of us, until Bob suggested that it was time to go to the pub. They made for the door. I said the things you're supposed to say; not 'Oh no, don't go, I'm loving it', but 'Nice to meet you' or something of that sort. Neil looked puzzled. 'You've got to come too', he said.

We spent the evening in the pub. Smoking yourself was the only way to prevent the opaque blue fog engendered by the other smokers from making your eyes run. Not that we needed that encouragement. The three of us were already heavy smokers. Then Neil set out for Finchley Road and Bob and I went home. An hour or so later the phone rang. It was Neil. The Australians had changed the lock and put his luggage on the landing. It was a matter of unpaid rent and a complete failure to wash up. Could he come and sleep on our sofa?

There followed one of the happiest weeks of my life. They finished the Tudor village. Bob returned to Wolverhampton. Neil and I spent every minute together. We went about London. We visited the Wallace Collection and ate at the café there because Neil had a ten-shilling note. When he couldn't immediately find it and started searching his pockets we looked at one another and simultaneously began to sing Debussy's 'The maid with the flaxen hair' in a wordless parody of restrained desperation, to which it lends itself remarkably well. We nearly went to Hampton Court but jumped off the bus – no closing doors, just an open platform – because we'd spotted 'Monsieur Hulot's Holiday' showing at a cinema en route. That gloriously funny film remains entangled with memories of dazed disbelief mixed with a sort of weightless exhilaration. This was not the Irishman in Verona. This was someone who enjoyed my company, who enjoyed being with me. At the end of the week Neil asked me to marry him. I said yes, of course. He was 21 to my 27. But he was six foot three with outrageously long hair (for 1954) and very handsome in a thin, helpless way; he was a talented designer, he improvised brilliant jazz on my Broadwood, and he was fun. What more d'you want?

Millie's cancer had suddenly taken her over. The wedding would be the last family occasion she was well enough to enjoy. She planned it all with such pleasure and Ern never complained about her extravagance. Though he did once tell us that he'd give us the money if we'd elope. It was only a joke, but looking back I can see that he feared for us. As Neil's mother said in her Liverpool accent when we went to tell her of our engagement, 'Aw soon, how're you going to manage?'

On the evening before the wedding Millie had arranged for our family doctor to come and talk to me about what I might expect, something she had never been able to do herself, apart from saying, from time to time, 'Men – useless animals. You'll see.' The school curriculum did not include sex education. And my reading was exclusively from the 19th century when, as everyone knows, they didn't have sex. Millie didn't think to mention this plan; it might have seemed reasonable to her at the time, but I don't know who was more embarrassed, he or I. I did at least have the pleasure of telling him that I was not a virgin. He made that sound that is a kind of abstract swearing and left.

Nothing could spoil that time. I made the wedding dresses for myself and the two small bridesmaids; Mary, my niece, and her best friend. Neil and I were married on 30th October, 1954, in St. Mary's Church, Wimbledon. After the reception at an hotel on Wimbledon Common we were delivered to the room with kitchen and use of bathroom that Neil had found in a Belsize Park basement, in one of those shiny black cars with white ribbons, a Rolls or a Bentley. He and Bob had stocked the kitchen, put flowers in the room. And there we spent our honeymoon.

VI

It was now that I began to understand the importance of money. Apparently you couldn't eat without it. I knew that, of course; but I had not so far experienced it. When our small store of it ran out we finished off the top tier of our three-tiered wedding cake which we were supposed to be saving for the christening and I developed a craving for pickled onions. Dear Neil. I discovered that I had married someone dangerously like myself. His outside person was much more convincing than mine. But if you'd sent a pair of ten-year-olds out into the world to live independently they might well have made a better job of it than we did.

He had already worked for a season at Gainsborough Rep and Bob had painted scenery at Worthing Rep; neither one of them had any qualifications – just a lot of talent. In those days that seemed to be all that was required. They had obtained the necessary Equity cards. They longed to work, regularly frequented the job centres – the Cranbourne pub near Leicester Square was a good one. Work remained elusive. Bob came to supper on one occasion and we sat over the meal, my two stage-designers and I, trying to think of a friend within walking distance who would lend him the bus-fare home. We walked a lot in those days. While I was at the Academy Bob and I, without a penny between us, once walked from Wimbledon to Baker Street to join a queue for a free student production of Britten's 'Albert Herring'. The 'house full' notice went up as we reached the front of the queue. We walked home.

Neil scanned 'The Stage' looking for work; it did not occur to me that I should look for some too. We went on borrowing and smoking with eating coming a poor second. Then a friend told Neil that Murreyfield Ice Rink in Edinburgh needed someone to do sound-control for its Christmas production of Chu Chin Chow on Ice. I don't think Neil knew a lot about sound-control, but the friend assured him that you could pick it up very quickly. He applied for the job and got it. I told you his outside person was more convincing than mine. He was to earn twelve pounds a week – a reasonable sum – but our room in Belsize Park cost four pounds a week and the room he found in Edinburgh four pounds a week, each; that included breakfast and an evening meal. I'm telling you this to set the scene at Euston Station. We were both wearing our 'going-away' clothes, the beautiful stuff we had changed into after the wedding. We were young and happy. 'Hold on', Neil said, as we were about to board the train. He dashed off and returned with Vogue magazine and some really extravagant flowers for me. You have to love him.

The enormous room in Mrs McGrail's tall, grey stone house, with the one-bar electric fire, was freezing; it was, after all, late December. Breakfast was tea, cornflakes and toast; the evening meal was a near-transparent slice of ham with some lettuce and half a tomato each. At Murrayfield Neil and I sat together in the little box overlooking the ice-rink, which was at least warm. He did indeed pick up sound-control very quickly. The main thing to avoid was heterodyne; one speaker could feed into another until between them they set up a howl which had people running from the auditorium. It nearly happened, but only once, when we had momentarily left the box during an interval. Neil leapt up the stairs, three at a time, ran at the panel of dials and managed to head it off.

The small orchestra sat in one corner of the rink on a triangular platform of wooden boards; sometimes they sounded as though they had finally succumbed to frost-bite. Neil once tried to cheer the M.D. by telling him how good the first act had sounded. The man replied – 'I know. The flautist was late'.

We had already survived the three shows on Christmas day when my father phoned me. As instructed, we had all been playing his chosen game; Millie was not to be told. Even when she had already been told. Ern could not bear to face this evident fact. As soon as she was first admitted to hospital and diagnosed with uterine cancer she sent for a priest. That was when it came home to me that she was a Catholic. She had lapsed so thoroughly on marrying Ern that we children had grown up assuming that fathers took you to church and mothers made the

Sunday lunch; I had hardly re-examined that conclusion. However, a priest was sent for. 'How long is it since your last confession, my child?' he asked her. According to Millie, she lay back on the pillow, laughing, and told him 'Thirty years'. He left. The man walked out on a dying woman who could still laugh but wanted absolution. The last rites. If only there were a God to make him know what he did. In my view he didn't deserve his faith, such as it was. Fortunately Vicky had married a Catholic, the man with the numerous problems. And he did this good thing. He found an Irish priest called Father Widderson who visited Millie regularly when she came home to the Wimbledon flat. He was a little eccentric. He was reputed to have shouted at a family of mourners attending their mother's funeral and sobbing so loudly that he couldn't make himself heard, 'That isn't your mother. That's just meat'. I doubt if it silenced them.

Now my father phoned. Millie didn't have very long. The doctor wanted her to be re-admitted to hospital and this was another thing he could not bear. Would I come home and look after her? Neil and I had been married for less than three months and I hope you will be appalled to learn that I went. I am. But Ern needed Millie so desperately. Near the end when a visiting friend of hers said, as people do say, 'It'll be a relief when it's all over' he replied 'No. As long as she's still here'. I heard the horror in his voice. At a time when she lay totally emaciated, unable to speak, take food or water; a collection of cells obstinately alive.

When the Murrayfield season ended Neil had come back to London, to live with me in the Wimbledon flat. Where else should he live? But the terrible game continued with its inevitable consequences. 'He's no good, he's not making a home for you, I don't need you here....' Et cetera. One of the few things that made her happy in those last five months — she would never have survived for five months in hospital, and rightly so — was Bob's success. He was to be the stage designer at the Pitlochrie festival that summer. She was so proud; if we were not to admit that her time was limited, Bob had very little choice. He left for Scotland.

Neil looked for work and I watched Millie die. Watched the tide of learned behaviour, tact, simple kindness, recede, driven back by pain, until all that was left was the longing. 'Why is it always the one you really want who is never with you?' she cried out once.

One morning I took a phone-call from Brighton for Bob. The theatre on the end of the pier – yes, that pier, the pretty one that burned down – needed a designer in a hurry. Was Bob available? No, I told them. And then, in an entirely uncharacteristic moment of daring, said 'But Neil Hobson is'. There followed eleven weeks in which Neil commuted to Brighton and I spent the weekends with him. It was where we first met Robin Ray, then a young actor with one line as a policeman in that week's play. What was known in the profession as a cough and a spit. We spent the day watching a magnificent beach-performer give his Mr Punch in a tiny traditional booth. The three of us spent hours leaning over the promenade railing watching a master at work; painting the scenery could wait. One night we slept on the stage, on a sofa under some heavy velvet curtains, dragged from the wings. There was only one simple back-cloth to paint, so Neil wrote on it in huge letters, 'Fireman. Please wake at 6.' The fireman always did a round at 6 a.m. and another at 9 a.m. That was when we finally came round. 'Why didn't you wake us?' Neil asked him; 'There's a rehearsal at 10'. 'You looked so peaceful', he said. We got it finished. Just. I painted the plain bits.

Millie died at last. It was hard to tell. She really looked no different. Ern was reduced to using a mirror to ascertain if she were still breathing. Bob came briefly from Pitlochrie and the funeral was held, but I didn't attend it. I cannot understand why, even now. There was no wake to prepare, no friends or wider family to welcome. But everyone else agreed that it would be for the best. So that was what happened.

RADA had acquired a new principal; John Fernald was a working director who shared his considerable talent between the West End theatre and the students. The gap between the two narrowed, to the great advantage of both in my view. Whole plays were mounted in the Vanburgh Theatre; I remember brilliant performances by Sian Phillips, Albert Finney, Peter O'Toole... I remember them because John, who could spot talent a mile off, had spotted Neil and appointed him Honorary Scenic Designer for RADA. The 'Honorary' referred to the very small salary; but it was a salary.

My father moved to live with Vicky and her family in Kent; Neil and I, with Judy, my mother's little white Pekingese, moved into a basement flat on Sylvan Hill, Crystal Palace. It sounds like the last act of a pantomime, but it did have certain defects; the two huge back rooms in this old Victorian house looked out onto a long sloping garden, but the front rooms were underground. Two brick-lined trenches under the windows prevented Sylvan Hill from moving in with us, but you could scrape the furry mould from the walls. We loved it. We didn't need the damp half; we lived happily in the two great rooms – a bed in one and the Broadwood in the other. It was probably better for the Broadwood than my present central heating. The bedroom had French windows opening onto the garden, the living room had a coal fire and a tall, walnut television set with a screen about half the size of the A4 on which I'm writing. (With a pen, of course. I'm from that generation). Bob maintained that we were so near to the Crystal Palace mast you could get a better picture if you stood in the garden and held up a plain postcard.

I subjected another group of defenceless children to my piano teaching in a Sydenham school and Neil worked at his design for the Big Break. John was directing a musical called 'Harmony Close' and he had entrusted the designing of it to Neil. In the evenings we worked on the scale models – model-making was a skill which I had to pick up very quickly. Half-inch-to-the-foot, they were, in those days, though I believe 1-to-30 centimetres is now more common. I simply loved doing it. I really took to it. There was just one problem. I found that I had married an owl, not a lark; Neil would never start work on a model until after about 10 o'clock in the evening. Later, if we'd been to see a film first. Then Bob would come round or our friend Dougie Heap, both prepared to work all night in an emergency. I'm a natural lark, and I never did quite get used to it; but I was amazed to find that the coming of the dawn – and it came at a point when standards were beginning to fall – miraculously revived us.

Robin was another frequent visitor. Another owl. We would huddle round the little fire, laughing and talking and arguing. Neil once maintained that anyone could play anything on the piano, given time. Robin bet him £5 that he couldn't play Ravel's 'Alborado del Gracioso' within six months. It's a beautiful piece – but difficult. Neil was getting work now, but he took the challenge seriously. He was doing really well with the fearsome double glissandi. We played together too. I remember a two-piano arrangement of Walton's 'Popular Song' from the Façade Suite which we played, of course, on the one piano we had. We planted runner beans in the garden, fell in love with Judy, who was a lively little animal, prepared to take on dogs of all sizes and not the lazy, snuffly stereotype you may imagine; we attended rehearsals and first nights; it was a good time.

VII

Neil began to suffer from bad headaches. He had had an abscess under a tooth which was treated, although the tooth was not removed. He was very resistant to the idea of seeing a doctor, but he did finally agree; a sinus infection was diagnosed, he took the antibiotics and things began to improve. We decided to visit his mother. We were drinking the first cup of tea of the day – we'd already smoked the first cigarette – looking forward to Liverpool and mother's Scouse, a thick, greyish stew of potatoes and onions (a lot) and lamb (not very much) eaten with mustard pickle. This is comfort food of a very high order. Try it. Neil was still in bed but I had got up to get a case and was sitting on the bed putting stuff for the weekend into it. We were talking about the effect of the first world war on men like my father and his – Neil's father had died in 1940 when he was eight years old.

Neil stopped talking in the middle of a sentence; after a second or two I looked up from my packing. He had fallen back onto the pillow and was shaking violently in some kind of convulsion. I threw myself at him, held him as tightly as I could and tried to make it stop. I willed it to stop. It didn't. I dialled 999 and called an ambulance, then I phoned the doctor He came at once, but by then this awful thing had disappeared. He examined Neil, but whatever he was looking for, he didn't find it. What I saw had left no trace. 'We'll let the ambulance come', he said. 'Just to be sure'. Then he left.

The ambulance came. The men took one look at Neil and laughed. 'We were expecting an old bloke', one of them said. 'Not a young chap like you. We brought a stretcher. I'm sure you'd rather walk to the ambulance'. 'Do what they said' I hissed at them under my breath.

Neil was taken to Hither Green Hospital. For two days he lay in an E.N.T. ward, under observation. Not a symptom appeared. I phoned at 8 a.m. and visited him when allowed. The doctors I questioned were beginning to talk vaguely of things that happen once in a lifetime and never recur; I understood that I was seen as an hysterical woman who had either over-reacted or actually made something up. When I phoned at 8 a.m. on the third day I was told that Neil was unconscious, they were transferring him to a neuro-surgical ward in the Brook Hospital, Shooters Hill, and that if I could get there in time I could go in the ambulance with him.

Young men were expected on H1 at the Brook Hospital. The ward was full of them. On June the eighth, 1957, there was no law about motor-cyclists wearing helmets. We did arrive together in the ambulance, but Neil was wheeled away from me at a run, so I was unable to prevent the attempt to admit him to H2, the female ward, on account of his long hair.

He went straight into surgery. The abscess had eaten its way upwards and broken into his brain; it flooded the surrounding fluid, leaving little pockets of infection as it went, and settled on the left side, where it did terrible damage. I apologise to any neurologist who reads this, but an autobiography is a point of view. That was how I saw it. A surgeon explained to me that he was making holes in Neil's skull, trying to track down the source of the infection. I still hadn't understood. 'But you can cure him, can't you?' I asked. 'Well', he said, evidently meaning to encourage me. 'I'd say we've got a fifty-fifty chance'.

You can't often remember the exact moment of a disillusion; they usually creep up on you. But I remember this one. Between one breath and the next doctors were no longer ten feet tall, of godlike status and able to cure anything. They made good or bad decisions, had more or less talent, like the rest of us. My respect for them increased considerably.

Neil was unconscious for a week. They shaved off his lovely hair and took him down to surgery, they filled his cerebral spinal fluid with penicillin by means of numerous lumbar punctures. I remember two nights I spent waiting there, one with his sister and one on my own on an actual bed in a mahogany cubicle. There was a knock on the door in the small hours. A nurse asked me 'Mrs Neil Comfort?' Between the two words Neil and Comfort my Neil died. To be resurrected by the second of them. Neil Comfort was a Neil who didn't make it.

There must have been other nights. I thought that if God did exist, Neil and I needed him; this was no time to be ashamed of foxhole Christianity. I tried to pray and felt ashamed anyway; not for trying, but for pretending to a faith which I didn't possess. I had ceased to believe in God when I ceased to believe in Father Christmas. The attempt was a fake.

After a week Neil regained consciousness and the damage to the left side of his brain became apparent. He had lost his speech; his right side was paralysed, his painting arm completely, his right leg partially. He was having frequent epileptic seizures. The surgeon – and the penicillin – had saved him, but the woman who understood what he needed if he was to have any tolerable quality of life was the sister on H1. Sister Lester was a tiny, ferocious Irish-woman with an admirable disregard for the rules. She put Neil in a separate side ward and told me that I could spend all day with him if I wished. This at a time when visiting was from 7 p.m. to 8 p.m. only; when visitors queued outside the ward to be admitted on the stroke of seven and were dismissed by a bell at eight.

My father dealt with the flat in Crystal Palace and rescued the Broadwood. Joan and her husband, witty Roger Woddis who wrote political satire in verse for the New Statesman, allowed me to disrupt their lives by offering me a room in their flat, a bus ride away from the Brook Hospital, and I spent the days with Neil.

Every now and then there was another operation as infection was discovered in another little curly fold of his brain. I think there were eight altogether. I remember Neil's surgeon, who had just investigated one such possibility, though he did not have much faith in its existence, walking towards me down the hospital corridor, straight from the theatre, dressed in white from his hat to his boots, smiling cheerfully. I waited to hear the good news. 'Well', he said. 'We struck oil'. Don't misunderstand me. This is not a criticism. I am so glad that there are people who can detach themselves sufficiently to cut someone's head open with a power-drill and poke about in it looking for things. I couldn't do it. Not to save my own life or anyone else's. Could you?

The last operation involved cutting an even larger hole in the left side of his skull to relieve the pressure on the brain. At least I think that was the objective. The bone was removed and saved, to be replaced later, leaving the hole like an enormous fontanel. His surgeon sewed the scalp together again, of course. But the left side of Neil's head, bristling with a fine fur of new hair, swelled alarmingly. By now I was somewhere beyond alarm. I sat with Neil in the little side-ward, looking for him in the wreckage. I wouldn't believe that he was not in there somewhere. When I was taken to meet a patient with similar brain-damage who made sounds that closely resembled words I was horrified. Neil had to be able to speak. I would make him speak. (This degree of delusional omnipotence may well be a common reaction. I do hope so). He could sometimes sing the words that he couldn't say if they occurred in a song he already knew. When his surgeon visited him Neil would sing 'Morning. Morning' pitched precisely as in the song from 'Singing in the Rain' – 'Good morning, good morning, we've danced the whole night through…'. Neil's mother had a remarkable repertoire of old music-hall songs which she would sing at the piano, and we had both learned the words of the best ones. Slowly, over months, normality became sitting with Neil in that side-ward, smoking and singing like a pair of drunks. When I ran out of songs I tried leaving the last word of a short sentence with only its initial sound. Picking up a brush, for instance, and saying over and over again, I'm going to brush my h…, I'm going to brush my h…'. Eventually he would finish the sentence with an approximation of 'hair'.

Treatment continued. At one point Neil developed septicaemia. As he began to recover Sister Lester broke more rules. He needed a higher-protein diet than the hospital could provide. If I would like to bring his lunch I could use the ward kitchen to heat things up. I did, of course – every day for quite a while. Neil's appetite was phenomenal; I cooked huge beef stews, giant meringues filled with cream and pineapple. He ate the lot. On another occasion hearing that Neil was missing Judy, our little white Pekinese, Sister Lester allowed me to smuggle the dog into the side-ward in a basket, covered with a scarf. By this time I had become such a fixture on H1 that a visitor, seeing me coming out of the kitchen, told me that she was going now, and would that be all right?

At last, after a year, Neil was discharged. I took this stranger home with me, still looking for the man I knew. He had a confused version of speech, epilepsy, he was full of anger and despair and had very little means of controlling either. Someone – it cannot have been me – found a room for us in Cheyne Row, the Broadwood was moved in, and we started our life together all over again.

VIII

Cheyne Row must sound like an ambitious address to anyone who knows London. I'm not sure how many of these elegant houses in Chelsea were even then partitioned into rooms with gas-ring and use of bathroom. Ours was. Actually we had two rooms on the first floor, leading into one another. A bedroom which could accommodate a double bed if you excluded every other item of furniture, and a large room with beautiful windows. The house was run by a good-hearted Indian woman who never quite understood how I had managed to make the gas-meter accept IOUs. I put the money back later, I promise you.

Things were bad. I'm wondering if you really want to know how bad. Neil would embark on long, meaningless explanations about, for instance, a box and the sun. He would become progressively more irritated as I failed to understand him and would finally hit out at me wildly. Once or twice he tried to strangle me, but fortunately this is really hard to do with one hand. These were not serious, adult attacks; they were random outbursts of a six-foot-three two year old in a tantrum. I hardly need to say that I had not the slightest idea of how to deal with any of it. I remember being told, while Neil was still in hospital, that most wives in a similar situation left their husbands, to be cared for in a home, presumably. Only now I understand that this was not the sad statistic I took it for but a suggestion, kindly meant. It was too soon. We had been married for just two years and eight months. It was too soon.

In Cheyne Row I came up with the following really bad ideas. 1, that Neil's illness was the worst thing that had ever happened to anyone and that consequently nothing bad should ever happen to him again, and 2, that most of Neil's behaviour was caused by his illness and some might have happened anyway; but as it was impossible to tell the difference, and to hold him responsible for something over which he had no control would be an appalling injustice, it should all be considered as the inevitable result of brain damage.

I wish the following words to be carved on my tombstone: 'She thought too much and came to all the wrong conclusions'.

Let me tell you about the good thing that happened in Cheyne Row. When the piano was first moved in, with a pile of my music, Neil wept for a hitherto unsuspected loss. He could not write, not because he was unused to using his left hand, but because he couldn't remember the shape of the letters; and he could not read. Now he found that he could not read music. I found my two books of Bach's organ music in the heap of music which had arrived with the piano; if he could just learn to read the single line of the pedal part with his left hand we could play duets again.

I swear it was the music of Bach that dragged him back into something approaching a life; it penetrated his brain and introduced the beginning of order; the beautiful logic of it reached the man I'd been looking for. It took time, but he did it. And we played, hour after hour, we played ourselves into a state of exhaustion. I don't believe my love for any other composer's music would have survived Neil's constant demands. But then other composers only reflect the most important thing; Bach is the thing itself. I know, I know. In my defence I call my old friend Marcus Aurelius: 'The universe is change, life is opinion'.

At some point I deceived myself into thinking that I could earn some money. I got a job giving group piano-lessons in a boys' school near Victoria. I didn't last long. I missed the whole first day; I had put sandwiches and a thermos next to Neil's chair and got as far as the door when he said 'I've taken all my pills'. To the end of his life he was reliant on a cocktail of anticonvulsants to control his newly acquired epilepsy. I didn't think he had taken them. But I couldn't remember how many were left in each bottle. What if he had? I promised not to leave if he would tell me the truth. I tried again next day, when I was entirely responsible for my own downfall. I arrived, late, to be told by an agitated head-master that the whole school was assembled to rehearse the end-of-term concert and he was waiting for me to accompany them. I apologised, resigned and left. It was all I could do.

I knew I should never have been awarded that L.R.A.M. I must have been required to read something at sight. Yes, I could play. But only from memory. I would not have been able to accompany them badly; I would not have been able to accompany them at all. I went home and resumed my efforts to prevent bad things happening to Neil.

I see that I've written about his anger but failed to mention mine. It was alive and well and doing what anger usually does when you've decided that it's unreasonable and are trying to suppress it; it had turned inwards and was lying in wait for the moment when it could do the most damage. That is, of course, how I see it fifty-five years later; then I was getting through the days somehow, anyhow, waiting for Neil's miracle recovery.

I soon discovered the thing that Neil wanted most of all. He wanted to appear normal. Physically disabled, of course; but in all other respects perfectly capable. It was a brave attempt. His speech was by now very convincing; if you listened to it as much as I did you would have heard how he could be easily diverted from one category of things to another; from hours to minutes, for instance. Four would become twenty; that's where they both were on the clock-face. If a conversation started to go seriously astray I was usually there to field. Always, at first.

I have never kept a diary, and by now you may well be confused by the sequence of events. I know I am. The missing piece of bone in Neil's skull was finally replaced about a year after it had been removed. This left him with a shallow indentation, mercifully covered by his hair. It had been shaved off so many times; all that pruning had produced a fine crop.

At some point in 1958 we moved to Maida Vale; a first floor flat in one of those cream-painted houses with a steep rise of stone steps to the front door. There were six houses, I think, all converted into flats with a communal garden. Neil was determined to return to his career as a stage-designer. He started to work again at RADA. I was somewhat distracted at the time by the discovery that I was pregnant. We were both delighted. What better proof of Neil's normality could there be?

Then John Fernald asked Neil to design his production of Ibsen's 'Ghosts' at The Old Vic. It was a risk that only a generous man like John would have taken. Bob and Dougie Heap had already been doing all the model making and scene-painting; 'Ghosts' could hardly have been a gloomier play, or matched Neil's mood more perfectly; he painted – with his left hand, of course – a brilliant setting in dull greens and thunderous purples; he designed the costumes; Bob, Dougie and I made the model, the two of them produced the ground-plan, Flora Robson played Mrs Alving and Neil's surgeon came to the first night. It was an impressive performance of normality. The reviews were splendid.

Neil continued to get work. He would stagger off to production conferences, unable to make notes, his speech less than reliable, his memory a hit and miss affair. His talent carried him through for a while. But looking back, how I admire his courage. His life was, by now, divided into two quite distinct halves. There was the limping stage-designer making a wonderful recovery; and there was the man with whom I was living, the one who emerged – who was bound to emerge – when the front door closed and we were alone together. There is a limit to anyone's self-control and Neil had reached his. In that unendurably stressful life which he was struggling to maintain every last bit of it was used up.

I had reached the seventh month of pregnancy. Neil became angry again, and hit out at me. I lost balance and fell heavily. A week later I went into hospital and gave birth to a dead baby. Christopher. He had been dead for a week, they said. They wouldn't let me see him; a doctor explained that it would be for the best, as he was too ….. 'macerated' I think was the word he used.

Neil was desperately sad. We mourned together. I understood, for the first time, those women who seem unable to conceive, who nowadays make one 'in-vitro' attempt after another. I would not have believed that the longing could be so powerful. Christopher had released something into my system that only a live, healthy baby could satisfy. I could not look at a pregnant woman; friends got used to hiding prams under the stairs when I visited them; a television film in which a baby was briefly wheeled past on the screen became 'that film with the baby'. My mother-in-law hoped, very reasonably, that I would now settle down, get a job and look after her son. But I was beyond the reach of common sense; I was driven by a ruthless determination to conceive again, and as soon as possible. I thought 'If I had been healthier he might have been stronger, he might have survived'. No one in the hospital had asked me if I smoked, but I decided to give it up anyway. I had made numerous attempts already – cigarettes were so expensive – but this was the one that worked. It was, of course, pure superstition on my part; the medical profession was not yet convinced by the results of Dr Doll's research and I had not even heard of it. I soon did, though. I found a job with the Medical Research Council, then on the corner of Queen Anne Street. Neil was still getting work; he was still relying on the support of our friends; I was still convinced that he would, in time, make a complete recovery. Not of course, physically; even I did not imagine that I could magic away paralysis. But the rest …? This in spite of the fact that I had been told no further recovery could be expected after two years.

I started work at the Medical Research Council, sitting in a tiny cubby hole, about the size of a telephone box, as a receptionist. Dr Doll arrived one morning. After a while I was asked to take some papers up to the meeting he was addressing: I opened the door of the conference room with its long mahogany table and was met with an impenetrable blue haze of cigarette smoke. Convincing that lot was going to take time.

After a few months I was promoted to the registry. This was a really pleasant job. I sat with about ten other women round another long mahogany table. Post came in; some I suppose was urgent, the rest we filed in the boxes which lined the walls. They may well be looking still for vital, misplaced correspondence. We relieved the boredom by reading out the tragic letters, the funny letters, or best of all, the letters that were both. I particularly enjoyed the one from a man who wanted to be taller. He had paid some charlatan with the letters H.Y.T.E. after his name and had still not grown another inch. 'Was there a way of shortening his feet? (If nothing could be done to increase his height).' I like a man with a sense of proportion.

They were all so friendly and so willing to help. Even when I started to put a bottle of milk and a bag of fruit on the table in front of me every morning they pretended to ignore the glorious fact that I was pregnant again and didn't dare to tell them in case disclosure could somehow bring on a miscarriage. One of them would always jump up and offer to climb the ladder to the highest files the moment I looked like trying it. I must have been about six months pregnant when I finally came out.

IX

Matthew was born in Paddington General Hospital on 7th March 1961. Large, healthy, normal. This was love in its most simple form; I loved him, he loved me. Or did when he noticed that I was the source of milk. In a bottle, sadly. My body had been cheated once and wasn't playing. Never played again, in fact. Nothing that the most determined nurse could devise to extract this treasure from me made the slightest difference. I was forced to feed Lucy, my last-born baby, with a teaspoon by a sister who 'would not have a bottle on her ward'. 'Breast is best', she chanted. Well yes… But I still felt that keeping the child alive was at least of equal importance.

After a fortnight in hospital – routine in those days – Neil and I took our son home to begin living out the customary triangle – a jealous man, a demanding baby and a woman discovering how lack of sleep will lower your standards. Don't misunderstand me. Neil loved Matthew. But he had had nearly four years of my undivided attention since that disastrous day in 1957 and he did not mean to part with it now. He set tests. He would wait until Matthew was roaring for milk or a clean nappy and then call for my help with something he could genuinely not do with one hand.

None of this could diminish my joy in my son. He actually was the most beautiful baby in the world. I was surprised to find that no one stopped me in the street when I wheeled him out in his pram. Had they not noticed? Yes, mothers are boring. But don't think we don't know; we just don't care. Our lust for praise for our offspring is stronger than any shame. Do remember that when you're told how well Persephone did in her Grade IV cello exam and would you like to hear her play? It may help you to be more ruthless. It is the only way to deal with this affliction. Not all mothers suffer from it, of course. You didn't. But then you had a genius on your hands.

I had assumed that a live, healthy baby, loved as I loved Matthew, would satisfy the longing I had felt since the death of Christopher. Not a bit of it. Soon I was thinking that I didn't want him to be an only child and I was already 35 ..... Neil would recover. He was already recovering. And working as a designer. Looking back I find this degree of self-deception impressive. Neil was working because of the huge amount of help that Bob and Dougie were still giving him. That was not and never had been a situation which could continue indefinitely.

I was pregnant with twins when Neil's agent, Olive Harding at MCA, phoned me. 'I'm sorry', she said. 'But I can't get him any more work. They all say the same thing. 'That's the man who's ill, isn't it'? I don't remember how I communicated this awful news to Neil. Carefully, I imagine. He had been angry and jealous. Now he was angry and jealous and in despair. He loved Matthew, now 17 months old, and our beautiful little daughters. I mean, of course, that they were beautiful to us. They had arrived late and large, Emma looking like an elderly bishop and Sarah, who had emerged feet first, like Winston Churchill. Emma was named after Jane Austen's Emma and Sarah because I'd always thought it a beautiful name. I do hope I allowed Neil some say in the matter.

We had not so far owned a washing machine – in common with many people in 1962. I had six dozen towelling nappies and a similar number of gauze ones for the three of them. Fewer would not have dried in time. We bought a 'twin-tub', a top-loading thing with different tubs for washing and spinning. You had to lift the nappies from one to the other with wooden tongs. That was Neil's job. He insisted. Wooden collapsible driers, recalcitrant as deck-chairs, stood in every room, in the bath, on the bed; we lived in a white forest of drying nappies. It was a pantomime. By the time Matthew was 2 and the twins nearly a year old he was racing round our one-bedroom flat in my glasses shouting 'Just coming! Just coming!' in a frenetic imitation of me.

No one in their right mind would have allowed themselves to become pregnant again. But as you may have suspected, I was not entirely in mine. After an early miscarriage (mourned by no one but Neil and me) I become pregnant again. My father, who had helped us so much, made one final effort. He bought us a house in Enfield, and we moved there to await the arrival of our youngest daughter, Lucy.

For us, Enfield was a lonely place. I introduced people in that street who had lived on it for twenty years or more. And we only stayed there for ten months. Our friends were all in London; the Broadwood (do you remember the Broadwood?) was stored in a barn belonging to Joan and Roger and they were selling their house. The buyers, not unnaturally, wanted the piano removed. We so nearly lost it. With a week to go we heard of a flat in Tulse Hill, South London; half the ground floor of a crumbling Victorian house with a 25ft. drawing-room, for a reasonable rent. I've promised to tell you everything, but I have to admit I'm ashamed of this bit; we sold my father's present and moved to Tulse Hill in time to rescue the Broadwood.

Re-reading the last couple of pages I see I have suggested that Neil's evident disabilities prevented him from continuing to work in the theatre. This is so far from being the truth – and just when I've reminded you of my promise to be honest about everything. I'll try. But it's difficult. A neurologist or a psycho-analyst would make a better job of it. Perhaps the fact that I'd probably need the two of them indicates where the problem lies.

Neil was a person with extensive brain-damage. His right side was partially paralysed – his painting arm totally; he was having severe epileptic seizures which made him irritable, irrational and sometimes violent in the hours before the attack and deeply depressed after it; he could neither read nor write to any useful degree; I needed to draw each letter in the air so that he could put 'Love from Dad' on a birthday card; his re-learned speech was not entirely under his control. But he was also a brilliant young man who at 25 had lost everything he had always taken for granted – his ability to use his talent, to play his beloved jazz, to speak with easy fluency and wit; he had lost the beautiful image of himself, the tall, handsome young man with the world opening up in front of him.

Now we were not alone. We had four small children. And Neil loved them. He was proud of them while he could still do things that they couldn't. But once their abilities exceeded his own he could not praise their achievements. He was too much like them to be anything but jealous. To the many friends who will say 'But Neil wasn't like that', I can only ask 'How do you know?'

One thing that Neil could and did share with his children was his love of music. I can see Emma at seven, standing by the piano while he improvised with his left hand, joining him on her recorder or singing away in a world of her own, one he had created for her. These were the good times.

Would you mind holding on to all this? Then I need only mention any relevant incidents, although the situation never changed. Neil seemed to have lost – one more loss – the power to change. He could not let go. He could not accept what had happened to him. He told me many times that no one could have done so. That in itself was a conviction which denied him peace. One of the things that I learned when it was no longer of any use, was this: if you live for 24 hours a day with someone whose mind does not work in the usual manner you will gradually acquire his way of thinking. At first, perhaps, you may pretend to agree, to avoid trouble; but sooner or later you will lose your sense of what is reasonable. Professionals go home at night. They have other lives which, with any luck, will anchor them in reality. I'm just telling you. It is a thing to be avoided. But professional help seems to have been in very short supply in the mid-sixties.

Which was when I became pregnant again. To those of you who are now asking 'Had this woman never heard of the pill?' I can only say yes, I know. It was the Swinging Sixties. I missed them. The doctor I saw put the matter very plainly. 'If you have another child you will break down. Then who is going to look after your husband and children?' I have strong views on abortion. It should be freely available to anyone who needs it; I agreed, with what reluctance you may imagine, to have one.

I had the breakdown all the same, though. It happened like this. After surviving the disapproval of the nurses on my ward I was sent for the routine visit to a psychiatrist. I wish I could remember his name; I would so love to thank him. He said 'You should be doing something besides playing super-mum. I think you should write. Write something and I'll see you next week'. I shouted at him 'When am I going to write'? There was no stopping him. 'Early, before the children wake up.'

I bought the cheapest paper I could find on the way home – that flimsy stuff which was used for copy-typing under a carbon paper. And a biro. I thought the idea ridiculous and yet I was disturbed by it. I had to try. The children usually woke up at about 6.30. So at five o'clock next morning I sat at the kitchen table with a blank sheet of paper in front of me. I stared at it. About my life, he had suggested. But how? How do you write? I put the pen down. Then something occurred to me, learned a lifetime ago in those Euclid theorems. Somewhere there must be that beautiful straight line which is the shortest distance between two points and I would look for it. I picked up the pen again and wrote: 'We were leaving the house in Wimbledon Park because the door handles squeaked. Or so my mother told me. I was four at the time and it seemed an adequate explanation.' What could I cut? 'Or'? No, I needed the 'Or' to suggest the alternative explanation, unsuitable for children. Could I lose 'at the time'? No, cutting that ruined the rhythm. I tried another sentence. Another page. By the time the children came looking for me I was hooked. Instantly and forever.

X

To be fair to that psychiatrist, he did suggest that I went to bed early; as I was going to get up early. That was the part of his advice that I failed to follow. Neil was watching more and more television; by now there was more of it available and it took the place of so many things. He watched it all day and late into the evening. What was more, he wanted me to watch it with him. When the children were finally persuaded to sleep and I had washed up it was his turn. His desire to have me constantly with him had grown into a need; its satisfaction could be postponed, but not indefinitely. As it grew, this need, the fear grew with it. The fear that I would leave him. No matter how often I told him that I would not, the fear remained. When it became unmanageably acute he would lock me in the room with him and pocket the key – if I wasn't quick enough to stop him. Social Services had awarded us a home-help for two hours, three times a week, and he maintained that they had only done this so that I could spend the time with him. The children, now 5, 3 and 2, would run up the long tiled corridor from the nursery and weep outside the door.

I too am appalled when I recall what I brought them into. But consider. They are loving, intelligent, funny, creative adults and – since you ask – they work their socks off contributing to society.

Tell me I shouldn't have had them.

To return to the promised breakdown. I continued to write. Gradually I found that doing ordinary things required a greater effort. Making a meal, for instance. Something resistant grew in my head. The anger was coming into its own. I could get half way across a room to perform a simple task and stand there unable to move. At last I could only lie on the floor and cry; Lucy, two years old, brought me pieces of toilet-paper to wipe my eyes. Someone must have called an ambulance, and on the twins' 4th birthday I was taken to the Bethlem Royal Psychiatric Hospital.

Depression was diagnosed. Such a soft word, a shallow, gently sloping hollow in a landscape. But depression is a sharp, hard thing, a pain in the head that you know doesn't exist; you're a fraud, and any moment now you'll be found out. It is not like being depressed as in 'Oh I'm so depressed'; it is not feeling down, or sad, or even deeply unhappy. You know those little wooden dogs made of separate pieces held together by a string which you can pull to tighten or loosen their joints? Well somebody's cut the string. Whatever it was you were using to make decisions and act on them, it's gone.

Meanwhile, in the real world, the Social Services had come up with a solution to a real problem. They had one home-help, an elderly lady, who was prepared to take on the whole family. Miss Bowes moved in. Predictably, the children hated her; I just added her to my burden of guilt.

The regime at the Bethlem was simple. Three pills a day, a fifty-minute hour with a psychotherapist once a week, group therapy and occupational therapy – this latter therapy was the best. I did pottery. I made a furious baby lying face-down, with clenched fists, kicking and – presumably – screaming. Well. I felt that it was expected of me. The daily dose of pills was increased to six a day. Then nine. Then twelve. My words came out in the wrong order but nothing else changed. Any true thing I told my nice young therapist was purely unintentional, but I'm sure he was doing very well without my help.

One thing had already changed, though. Some detached part of me was observing my fellow patients like a child in a sweet shop. As I said to a visiting friend, 'Honestly Gerald, this place is a madhouse'. I started to make notes. I had them spread all over the table in the ladies' lounge one day, trying to arrange them in a coherent order, when my therapist came in search of a reluctant patient. He looked at my scraps of paper and his young face said 'As long as it keeps her happy'. I thought 'You wait'. It gave me fresh energy. Proving him wrong would be such a pleasure. Him and his good job and his good suit and his sensible life.

After about two months, a fruit bowl and several more clay figures, I was asked if I would give my consent to E.C.T. Electro-convulsive Therapy. I said that I would. I cannot for the life of me remember why;

some lunatic self-destructive urge, no doubt. I had seen patients after E.C.T. Happily the plan was abandoned and after another month I was discharged.

A year later I was back. I think it was the weight of my promise to the children that I would never leave them again that did it. A promise acknowledges the possibility of failure – why, otherwise, would you need to make it?

Once again Miss Bowes moved in and I began to see that this might well turn out to be my annual holiday. The pills didn't work. I decided to ask for help as an outpatient. In case you are now thinking 'Ha! You'll be lucky', I was lucky. I had two years of psychotherapy with the same therapist, but at the Maudsley Hospital, once a week. It did leave me with the conviction that I had no bad problems, only bad reactions to them, but it kept me out of the Bethlem. I never went back.

As the children grew up they instinctively followed my unspoken law; they too had sensed Neil's desperate need to present himself to the world as other than he was. The world on the other side of the front door, that is. The rest was strictly between ourselves. Writing that still feels like a betrayal. And yet how could a badly brain-damaged man be expected to behave? Badly. Particularly in the long period building up to an epileptic seizure, Neil still became irritable, then irrational, then angry. And his anger, once released, was still uncontrollable.

He loved our children. But they were learning to do so many things that he couldn't. He could paint though. For a while he did. I loved those left-handed paintings. They had lost everything easy, automatic, conventional; every mark, every line was meant to be there. I still have one of them, framed and hung – a row of suburban houses, spiked with aerials beneath a purple-grey sky. In ink and wash, his favourite medium. The bottom half of our large garden had been bought by the council and left; I don't know how many years it took for the trees and bushes to take over and the blackberries to fill in the gaps, but the children called it 'the forest'. By then we had removed the remains of a wire fence. I once went looking for them and found a pear tree with golden fruit, some ripe, some rotting around its roots, which I had never seen. Neil painted the forest in all its seasons. I wish I still had those four pictures. They were sold to a friend who thought them over-priced – they were not.

Eventually music overtook even painting. He had developed a remarkable left-hand piano technique and would improvise by the hour. Jazz, Gershwin songs, wonderful thirties stuff. Ronnie Cass, a musician friend who could turn his hand to anything, listened, wrote what Neil played, and for some years copies of Neil's arrangements could be bought at the Disabled Living Foundation in central London. I hope someone out there is still enjoying them. These were the good times, in between the others, when Neil would play, Emma would sing, and what she had not already inherited of his ear for harmony she absorbed. I did try to teach all four of them to play the piano in my more formal way, but it was clear that they hated to see me in that role. So I limited my contribution to 'you could try a fourth finger on the B flat' as I walked past the door. That worked.

I was forty-six when Bob had his best idea ever. He would give me driving lessons and a car when I'd passed the test. I may actually have been the person least likely to. I have no spatial awareness whatsoever and no sense of direction. It took fifty lessons and three tests; I only passed then by taking one of Neil's valium tablets. Half a tablet. I tried it out with my driving instructor first, and a whole one left me dangerously carefree. My first instructor had stopped the car with his dual-controls after ten minutes and asked me 'Do you think you're going to be able to do this'? Remember Bob Newheart's 'The Driving Instructor' and feel for the man.

The new car arrived. After a week of terror, swooping too fast around corners in no gear at all because I couldn't remember the right one, I loved driving. I'd have given it up during that first week but the prize was too great – and then I loved it. Neil was a challenging passenger. On the good days we took coffee, Gray Dunn's caramel wafers, and drove off to the countryside while the children were at school. On the less good ones he would bang in rage on the left hand window and shout 'Right!' I once hit a taxi in the moment of indecision that this could cause. Or, if he became really angry, he would sing at the top of his voice in a kind of wordless insult, loud enough in that tiny space to unhinge the most careful driver.

The children kept me sane. They were stoical about not going on school trips, but there was no avoiding the eight o'clock tax. 'We've got to have a pound each to wear our own clothes today and on Monday we've got to come as rock-stars/spacemen/wearing green. School uniform was free for those on benefit. Matthew suggested buying Emma a new blazer she didn't need and selling it to pay for the required calculator, new, expensive, and not free to those on benefit. Bad or not, it was my choice. And I am glad that I didn't leave Neil alone with his sandwiches to go out and earn an honest, childless living. We were a family, if we did feel more like survivors in a life-boat with the water running out.

Now that I could drive, it was suggested that music therapy might be helpful to Neil. I could take him to Earls Court once a week to see Mary Priestley, daughter of the writer, violinist and fine, if eccentric, music therapist. On the appointed day I took Neil to Earls Court and, with fifty minutes to wait, found the nearest café – the ABC then opposite Earls Court Station. I sat in the middle of a chattering, tea-drinking crowd, not one of whom needed me. I was to be alone. Every week. For nearly an hour. I remembered the notes I'd made in the Bethlem.

XI

I had heard somewhere that the second book was the hardest to write; you'd squandered all your material in the first one. I had already written the first book in those early mornings which, together with my reluctant abortion and one or two other things, had resulted in depression. I determined to consider my second book as the first. I kept the earlier one for years, never re-read it and finally threw it away. The depression was the best thing that ever happened to me; but throwing away the first book comes a close second. The depression because everything broke out of the box and there was no getting it back in again; the disposal of that book because it let me free to use whatever material I wanted to, but differently. Every now and then an accurate phrase or an accidental moment of honesty would surface and be re-used, but when I sat down to write in the Aerated Bread Company I started all over again. It was noisy, and I had only what was left of an hour when I'd managed to park the car and queued for tea and a bun. But I learned a useful skill from those restrictions. I didn't hang around for inspiration; I used whatever time was available. Even with all the time in the world (until it finally runs out) I can still sit at my writing table and say 'forty-five minutes starting........now'.

Neil continued to benefit from music-therapy and I continued to write, once a week, perhaps for a year or more. As Jane Austen says of quite a different matter, 'I only entreat everybody to believe that exactly at the time when it was quite natural that it should be so, and not a week earlier' the house subsided, suddenly and with a sound like a gunshot. A huge crack appeared over the drawing-room door and the long tiled corridor developed a slight but alarming slope. Worse, the beautiful Victorian ceiling in the drawing-room, heavy with plaster wreaths and flowers, began to lose its grip. Small warning chunks fell from time to time. We had to move.

The house at the top of the hill behind the Horniman Museum was one of six just built by a housing association for families with four children. We moved in on Christmas Eve, why, I don't recall. Matthew and I – he would have been about fourteen – raced round a near-empty Sainsbury's and filled a trolley with anything that looked like Christmas. The day itself was memorably bad; it gave rise to the phrase 'Dad's in his holiday mood'. Ignoring the behaviour recommended for use in these circumstances by Dickens, Neil said the steak was inedibly tough – it was – and became very angry with a childish disappointment only touching in retrospect; then retired to the living room, above the kitchen in this tall town-house, to watch television. Such separation was becoming a pattern. Howard, a constant and generous friend, had made us a pine trestle-table, and we bought two pews for a very small sum from a vicar who had better plans for the space they occupied. I cooked and washed up and sorted the piles of dirty clothes to the ritual chant of 'delicate light, delicate dark'...... and the children sat at the table on the pews, near enough in age to laugh and talk together. The five of us developed a black humour which, when any two of us get together, can still shock strangers.

Music therapy had moved with us. I covered the walls of the garage with thick dark brown slabs of cheap packing-cork, someone gave us a lime-green sofa, Howard built cupboards and a work-surface in front of the permanently closed garage door and the Musicians Benevolent Fund provided an upright piano. Neil began to work with the little son of a friend, a six-year-old boy with severe learning difficulties and a strong sense of rhythm. Neil would play and the little boy would accompany him on the few percussion instruments we could muster. It gave Neil the very thing he longed for – status in the outside world. But as he began to work with more children the strain on him became apparent. He could improvise but he could not move on. Every time was the first time. He poured out rhythms, harmonies, he poured out the small amount of peace he had acquired, at enormous cost to himself. The rest of us didn't do too well out of it either. We had been living on very little before, but now there were expensive pieces of equipment, a xylophone, drums, a cassette-recorder, that Neil insisted were essential to his work. We borrowed from the bank without a hope of repaying the money. He believed in his expanding career and

I did the talking. Why? you are probably asking. Because if he could have spoken easily and fluently it was what he would have said; if I had refused to speak for him I would have been depriving him of the right to a voice. I told you I thought too much.

Neil was no longer going to Earls Court once a week; he had started to work with young people in one of the local residential care homes. And I discovered the Horniman Museum. At the top of a wooden spiral staircase I found the old reference library and reading-room. It had heavy mahogany tables, comfortable chairs, and I don't believe I ever saw anyone there apart from the librarian. In this luxurious silence I wrote and wrote. I so detached myself from anything but writing that on one occasion I momentarily failed to recognise Emma and Sarah who had walked down through the Horniman Gardens to stand me tea in the café.

Eventually I found a way of finishing the book. What to do with it now? Bob had it typed for me, and I sent it to John Cornwell, the only writer I had actually met – on my rare visits to my brother and his wife. I needed an honest opinion and I felt that I could trust him to give me one. Then if the book was rubbish I could crawl into a hole and pull the lid down after me. Actually he wrote me an encouraging letter. And he did better than that. He sent the book to his agents.

I remember in vivid detail the moment when their letter arrived. The carpet from which I bent to pick it up, greyish-green with a faint muddy footmark. The thick, expensive paper in my fingers as I tore the letter open and forced my eyes to take in the whole content at a glance. A.M. Heath would like to represent me and would I ring to arrange a meeting. Nothing ever surpassed that moment. Not even when, a year later, I received a phone-call from the lovely woman who had become my agent, telling me that Heinemann, like all the other publishers she had tried, had said well, yes, but is there likely to be a second book? And on hearing that 'Oh Lily' was already written, had taken both books, with an option on the next two. No. It was that first letter. There was someone out there whom I had never met, who didn't know me or Neil or the children. Only what I had written. I had made contact. I felt like a miner in a pit-disaster who had finally heard a voice.

I had originally called the first book 'The Patient'. All of us, sitting in the Bethlem, patiently waiting for someone else to solve our problems, it meant to me. My agent was wiser. 'You need something to catch the attention' she said. I remembered Gerald, visiting me in the Bethlem as a woman kicked a metal waste-paper basket down the corridor because no one would give her a cigarette. 'What about "This Place is a Madhouse"?' I suggested. And this was the title adopted.

It came out, to good reviews. 'Oh Lily' was published a year later. John Osborne, briefly critic for the Evening Standard, gave me half a page with my photograph. I was immensely proud of the fact that he had enjoyed it. It was more than Neil could bear. He had lost the ability to use his real talent and the pain of that loss was still as acute at forty-eight as it had been at twenty-five. He asked me if I would stop writing now. I did contemplate it. But only for a moment. I told him that I would not.

Matthew was now twenty and working as a courier on a motorbike. He had started the second year of A levels, left for his grammar school one morning and returned an hour later. 'That's it', he said 'I'm going to get a job'. I think he hated school as much as I had. His peers said he talked posh; he wrecked his vowels in an attempt to accommodate their snobbery but it didn't help. The bikers were the first to accept him. A genuine community is a rare thing but bikers have one and Matthew's allegiance to it was immediate. I thought of Conrad Lorenz, those little chickens following a cat and knew that this I would have to accept. Ferocious looking bikers parked their bikes, crowded onto the pews, all black leather and chains, and asked 'Could I have another piece of cake please Mrs H?' Those were good days.

We were waiting for him to come home before we started on the special supper I had made to celebrate my 55th birthday when the police rang. He was unconscious in the Royal Free Hospital in North London. An elderly lady had walked out into the road in front of him, he had swerved to avoid her and hit a tree with his head. No, they could not tell me how serious it was. I drove Neil to the hospital talking myself loudly through every manoeuvre – 'Red light. Stop ...'

He was unconscious for 48 hours. When he came round he was revealed to be physically able but talking like a child who had not quite learned how. After a week he had had enough. He walked out. In his slippers and hospital pyjamas. In spite of his badly grazed face and his plastic identity wrist-band he got as far as Waterloo Bridge before a policeman stopped him. 'Where are you going, son?' he asked. 'Home' Matthew said. They put him in a cell with a friendly cop, tea and buns and a blanket, until I came to collect him. I took him to the hospital to be discharged but I'd had to promise I'd take him home to get him into the car. And I did.

It took him two years to recover fully. I told the girls not to humour him, not to laugh at his childish jokes, to stamp on anything that didn't look like Matthew. He sat in his room a lot when he realised how far he had to go. I know it sounds brutal but I wasn't going down the same road twice. And it worked. We got him back. Our courier on a motor-bike.

In the following year my father died. At ninety-three. Almost completely blind, intellectually undamaged and physically strong. He had the first stroke when he was working in his vegetable garden and, after three days of mild confusion, the final one. It was an ideal death. At home, where he had lived with Vicky and her family since Millie died. In the little room that smelt of cigar-smoke and, on that hot summer day, roses – their scent drifted in at the open window. He had survived the horrors of the first world war, the loss of his ambition, the loss of his wife, even the loss of his beloved Vicky, four years earlier. But Bob and I were there. I took him in my arms when his breathing changed; I felt his heart give one last thump – a Victorian who had lived to see men walk on the moon.

The evening of his funeral was less than ideal. I had driven down to Kent to attend it and returned to find that Bob, thinking I looked tired, had phoned and suggested that I come and stay in Oxford for a day or two. Neil was waiting for me in an irrational frenzy; he accused me of incest. This was too much for Emma, who was with us in the kitchen. She picked up a knife from the draining-board and went for him. My passionate, protective Emma. I managed to intervene, but the rest of the evening was spent taking her to stay with a friend. Till things quietened down. I went to bed when I came home but Neil would not let me sleep. He kept shouting about incest and pulling off the duvet. I ended up sitting on the stairs, wrapped in the thing, while Matthew, still not fully recovered from his accident, reasoned quietly and patiently in the bedroom. I heard him saying, over and over again between the shouting, 'No Dad, it's not like that Dad, it's just that Mum's tired and Bob thought ...' I brought my children into this chaos and they helped me survive it.

In the autumn the third novel was published. 'Poor Tom'. Something in Neil had taken a new direction. He had acquired a cassio calculator, a hand-held thing about a foot long; it had a mini keyboard with numbered keys. He spent more and more of his time recording random numbers from the television – the date, the time of a programme, a statistic about the migration of birds. He searched the Guardian for lists of numbers; page-numbers from an index were important. He sat in bed next to me with his cassio and fell asleep with it in his hand, presumably from exhaustion. Nothing I could say would persuade him to stop. From these numbers he would deduce unknowable facts. The Falklands war didn't happen; there had been a government plot to make us think it had happened. Grace Kelly hadn't died (he loved the film actress Grace Kelly). I thought it a very nice kind of madness that he should unhappen bad things. But then he told me that I shouldn't speak so loudly; the room was bugged because he was being tried out for MI5. He began to hallucinate.

I went to see the doctor, of course. This was when I discovered two important things. First, that our cover-up had been more successful than I realised, and second, that the depression on my medical record had invalidated everything I said. The doctor clearly regarded this as further evidence of my own problem. With difficulty I told him of the phone call Neil said he had received in which he heard my voice saying 'seventy times seven'. With difficulty because I had been so moved by this biblical reference to forgiveness and anyway which of us needed it most was none of his damn business. However, it did at least persuade him to come and see Neil.

His approach was jovial. 'What's this I hear about a phone call and seventy times seven?' he asked Neil, and waited for the fantasy to be dismissed. 'Yes', Neil said seriously. 'I heard it'. The doctor asked me to leave them. After a brief interval he came downstairs to the kitchen where I was waiting. 'Well, he's hallucinating all right'. 'So what can we do?' 'Wait till he gets worse', he said with a laugh and left.

I phoned Neil's surgeon, with whom we had remained on friendly terms. He had retired and was living in the country. 'I'll come up and see him' he said. After a long talk with Neil he was worried for the girls. 'They shouldn't be here', he said. Neil would never have hurt them. He loved them. But now, suddenly, there seemed nothing familiar or predictable left. We needed to make new plans.

XII

Finding somewhere in a hurry for the three of them to live resulted in one unfortunate relationship, one friend for life and the disapproval of a kind and well-meaning family who had, understandably, because I hadn't told them, no idea why all this was necessary. 'Why don't you go and see your father' they exhorted Lucy, repeatedly. 'He's not well'. Apart from phoning this family with my prepared explanation, it seems to me that I had very little to do with finding anything. The twins were as shocked and saddened as all of us by this new turn of events, but twenty chaotic years had made them resourceful; they bundled their possessions into carrier bags and off they went. What it cost them is another story, not mine to tell.

Matthew and I considered how we might persuade Neil to go into the Maudsley. This he refused to do on the grounds that it was not he who needed help. I had phoned every mental health organisation I could think of and discovered that there was no way in which we could insist on his being admitted unless, as far as I could make out, he was likely to harm himself or others. He was up there in the living room covering the margins of the Guardian with numbers. Not suicidal. I suggested provoking an attack – it would have been so easy – with Matthew standing by to rescue me, but he wouldn't hear of it. At last we decided that the only thing to do was to leave. Both of us. Neil was not capable of looking after himself; when we informed the social and medical services that we had abandoned him they would be forced to ensure that he got the help he needed. In the Maudsley. There was only one flaw; I couldn't do it.

I had been on a waiting list for a minor operation for about two years; it was nothing that couldn't wait another two and I had forgotten all about it. But it was then, while Matthew was trying to persuade me, that a letter arrived offering me an appointment in a few days' time. Two weeks in hospital. A reason to leave, but not for ever. It overcame my resistance. The naivety of our misplaced confidence is staggering, but we believed that Neil would get immediate help. I told him that I was to have this minor operation and left. Matthew saw me off; I suspect that he didn't trust me to leave if he went first.

The moment I was admitted to a ward I started to phone. I stood in the corridor – no mobiles – and rang one number after another on my list. Then I lay back in bed to experience two glorious weeks in which I wouldn't be allowed to get out of it. I had explained the help that Neil would need; now I waited for it to appear. Surely it couldn't take more than a day or two?

On the following morning Emma came to visit me. She brought a great fat Penguin novel. 'Here you are mum – you'll never get a better chance to read 'War and Peace'. I had not read since my marriage; Neil didn't read before his illness and after it he couldn't. I could have refused to watch television with him, sat in the bedroom and read. But I didn't. All that compulsive reading of 19th century novels in my childhood had lain dormant, rotted down into a compost heap of words and waited for this moment. I read like a starving man eats. Quickly. I read all day and until the lights were turned out at night, ignoring the other three patients in the ward, eating anything when I had to, only longing to get back to it. I worked at remembering the names and patronymics; I drew a map of the battle of Borodino – the paperback didn't have one. This was what a novel should be. I relived the old pleasure of Dickens and Scott and Trollope, but something else had got hold of me. This was the best novel ever written. Thirty years later I still think so. Not for the style of its prose or its theorising but for the world-creating wholeness of it. When I finished it I felt as though all my friends had emigrated. Would little Nikolai follow Pierre? He was clearly engaged in something important, even dangerous, and Nikolai sensed it. Would the marriage of Pierre and Natasha survive Tolstoy's imposition of his metaphor for female genital mutilation? Did he really believe this change in Natasha to be not only inevitable but desirable – and permanent? His ideal in a mature woman? I needed to know.

I thought of nothing else for three days. On the third night I woke up in the imperfect hospital darkness and thought: 'I haven't read it at all. I've read a translation. I will never, ever read this book in the original language. As Tolstoy wrote it.' I felt excluded from his world and it was unbearable. Nothing for it. I would have to learn Russian.

My two weeks in hospital came to an end. Matthew had visited me. It appeared that my phone-calls to the social services had been ignored. Horrified neighbours had brought food, helped him in every possible way except the important one; with the best of intentions they had enabled him to stay there alone in a state which even now I cannot bear to imagine. The decision to be made now was worse than the first one. Should I go back and try to live with his hallucinations and his unpredictable violence? And if I did, what chance would there be of his getting help then? I had tried everything I knew; the doctor, the social services, the numerous mental health organisations. Ours was the only way and it had to work. I decided not to go back. Not yet.

I went, instead, to my brother and his wife in Oxfordshire. Matthew drove me to their beautiful great house, Woodperry, and I spent several weeks with them. I still remember, with affection, how kind and gentle Jill was – Jill the barrister, whose mother once said to her 'why is it they always give you the innocent ones dear'? Jill, who I'm sure must have terrified judges. Bob came down at the weekends, but he was never a man to invite confidences. When Lucy visited me, desperately unhappy, I told her that I'd come back to London as soon as I could and we'd find somewhere together. After a day or two, Bob and I travelled together to London in his car; it would be the perfect chance to talk to him. And we did talk. All the way. About, among other things, the armour in the Wallace Collection. Dear Bob, I did love him. So did Jill. But he was too well defended. Like his beloved P.G. Wodehouse, he chose not to 'dig around in the depths' like Dostoevsky, but to 'see life as a musical comedy without music.' He was good company though. The best.

When I arrived in London I phoned Howard – auto-didact Howard, who could make anything in wood from a guitar to a roof-extension – and his darling wife Eve. I knew that they would put us up until we could find somewhere to live. So they would have done, had they been at home. Why I had not phoned them before I left Oxford is hard to understand. But all this is – what did Wordsworth call it?

'Emotion recollected in tranquillity'? At the time I was hanging on by the skin of my teeth to a situation getting rapidly out of hand.

Sarah was by now working in 'Next' and had rented a room in Catford. She and Lucy met me in 'The Chelsea', a little café in the shopping centre. One of them went out to buy a local paper and we looked for a room to rent. They all required a month's rent in advance, which we didn't have. After we'd made our toasted tea-cakes last for an hour or more it began to get dark. Every time I see a homeless person asleep in the doorway of a shop I think of that moment and know how lucky I am.

Sarah took us home to her room in Inchmery Road and persuaded the landlady to let us stay. Just for one night. And then just for one more night. The room for which she was taking money was somewhere between damp and wet; she was evidently not a woman with scruples. However, I'll give her the benefit of the doubt and say that she may have been persuaded by my crutches. Ah. I forgot to mention that the operation had been on both feet and necessitated plaster up to the knees for three months. Wooden rockers had been attached to the soles of the plaster which enabled me to walk with the aid of crutches though I soon got quite good at it without them. Whether they had moved the landlady to perform this good deed I can't now remember, but I'm sure I was using them ruthlessly. What I do remember is the duvet. It was as heavy as a sack of wet seaweed, which it closely resembled.

Then we met with one of those rare, beautiful people – a thoroughly good woman, the kind you never forget. Mrs Hayes, an elderly widow who lived at 15, Vancouver Road, somewhere between Catford and Sydenham, in case any of her grandchildren are listening. I'd love them to know. Hers was just another advertisement in the local paper. But when I spoke to her she said she was sure she could trust us and never mind the deposit. She showed us the bedroom with two single beds, a gas-fire and a television set; and the kitchen, with a big table and a real cooker. She must at one time have been connected to a carpet salesman – Mr Hayes, perhaps? because the hall and the stairs up to our rooms were wondrously carpeted with 18 inch square samples of every conceivable colour. Her own room – at the back of the house, to the right of the staircase, never saw daylight. Mrs Hayes had been a soubrette on the halls, later in variety, and artificial light preserved past successes; a bright orange stage-curtain effectively excluded the natural sort. A photograph of her wearing the very skimpy uniform of a maid in cap and apron, leaning forward from the waist in that arched-back pose, with a feather duster poised for action, hung on the wall amongst generations of variety artists. Her pride was a signed photograph from Larry Grayson.

Once a year she attended a dinner given in honour of the 'Lady-Ratlings' by the variety theatre's own charity whose members were known as 'The Rats'. I hope they still are, them and their King Rat; I know that they do a lot of valuable work for sick children. Lucy and I were lucky enough to be there as Mrs Hayes prepared for this event. She had asked us if we would come down at 6 p.m. and take her photograph. She was wearing a full length crepe dress in a vivid purple with one long sleeve and one bare shoulder. The bare arm was covered by a purple glove. Her white hair must have been dressed earlier. She looked magnificent. Then, as Lucy prepared to press the button she struck a pose from her repertoire, breathtakingly provocative. How I love that woman. You will not see her like again.

Lucy and I settled down to our ramshackle domestic life. She found herself an evening job at Casey Jones on Victoria Station. The competition was strong; she had to sit a written examination with a dozen other applicants, answering questions of the 'Why do you think you'd be good at this job'? variety. They should have tested their boredom threshold; stood them in a row handing out burgers and chips whenever a bell rang. Last one still standing to get the job. I'm proud to say that Lucy got it anyway. And it did have one great advantage; she would come back at midnight with the unsold cream doughnuts. Huge things, they were, a good nine inches long and oozing with cream and jam.

When, finally, my plasters were removed, I too went to the job centre. It was no easier to get a job at 56 than it is now but money was required. I didn't tell them about my un-earned LRAM. 'Anything', I said. The woman behind the desk gave me the form for the indecisive – an alphabetical list of all the jobs I might choose to apply for. But I only got as far as 'C'. Conductor, it suggested. a) Music, b) Bus. To use an old theatrical expression, I corpsed. That is, I broke into inappropriate and uncontrollable laughter. It cheered the place up a bit but the woman was cross. 'This is a serious matter' she said. That only made it worse. She threatened to have me removed, so I made one last effort and ticked 'Filing Clerk'. I didn't get a job though. Lady-Ratling or not, Mrs Hayes was a one-woman charitable organisation. Lucy and I were eligible for two kinds of welfare benefit in this generous country of ours – living expenses and a rent allowance. The latter would take another month or so, we were told. If we paid the rent we wouldn't eat; except of course, for the cream doughnuts. Mrs Hayes said the rent could wait.

In the end our plan worked. Neil agreed to be admitted to the Maudsley. It took a month, but it worked. He started to receive the necessary treatment, Lucy kept selling the burgers and I began another novel. It seemed the only thing to do in the circumstances. When after some months, Neil was discharged, the housing association placed another tenant in the house who undertook to look after him. The poor woman didn't last long. Neither she nor the landlords had any idea of what this might involve.

Matthew covered for me while I made the decision. After all, I argued, I had only left so that Neil would agree to go into the Maudsley. He had done what I'd asked. He sent me a message to remind me of my promise, not one I remembered making, but surely implicit in my intention of spending 'two weeks' in hospital, all I had ever discussed with him. The message ended 'would I come back now'? I went back.

XIII

I went back; but now it was different. How could it not be? True, Neil was no longer hallucinating – I think; but he was still relying on numbers. They had become a comforting psychotic bolt-hole that remained with him till the end of his life. It was I who had changed. Physical distance had enabled me to take a clearer look at what I was doing – it usually does. Now I see – and half-saw then – that once I had refused to stop writing change was inevitable.

I had not forgotten 'War and Peace'. As soon as I returned to the house in Horniman Drive I enrolled at Goldsmith's College in New Cross and signed up to attend evening classes in Russian. I would probably have been attending them still had it not been for an amazing piece of good-fortune. When Lucy and I left Mrs Hayes and Vancouver Road, she went to Bristol, where she worked as a Community Service Volunteer. After six months she returned to London and decided to study catering at SELTEC – South East London Technical College – briefly staying at home while she searched for a bedsit. On the list of such places provided by the college was an address in Sydenham.

I would like to say at this point that I had long since abandoned hope of a tidy home. My place was a tip. Mostly clean, but a tip. The house in Sydenham was in a different league. Mrs Behr lived in two houses knocked into one, threaded by two narrow staircases, with a huge wild garden. She had five elderly incontinent dogs for whom the doors were left permanently open; a seat at the bus stop was warmer, in winter, than the hairy sofa in her living room. Lucy only lasted two weeks there; Mrs Behr became a friend for life. As we left on that first visit she asked me 'Have you read this book'? I hadn't. 'Borrow it. You'll enjoy it'.

I read it. I did enjoy it. Then I had to take it back. There was something soft about her final consonants, something not quite English. But her grammar was perfect, her accent was perfect. Scandinavian perhaps? I hadn't got round to asking her when I told her about my plan to study the Russian language in evening classes. 'Don't do that', she said, disdainful and slightly puzzled by this stupid and unnecessary idea. 'I'll teach you'. Only then I discovered that Tatiana Borisovna was Russian, that she was born Zakharova; that her father, Boris Zakharov, had studied with Sergei Prokofiev at the Petersburg Conservatoire and her mother was a violinist with an international reputation, now retired and living in Germany.

When Tatiana was four, in 1921, she was woken one night, dressed in two coats, given a ball to hold and told that they were going to play in the park. The family left the rigors of post-revolutionary Petersburg, left the great house on Griboyedov Canal and made it across the Gulf to Finland in a small boat. From there they travelled to Paris, where Tatiana grew up. At eighteen her father, now a much-loved stepfather, a German philosopher, told her that her behaviour was too Russian. This she once defined to me as talking all night and not doing anything. This, at least, was what he meant. He sent her to England, where she added English to her Russian, French and German, then took a degree at Oxford in languages. If I had tried to invent a Russian teacher I would hardly have dared to invent Tatiana – or Tatisha, as she was always known. Her French school-friends called her 'Tati' and her Russian ones added the 'sha' as being more like a proper Russian name.

She wouldn't accept any payment for my lessons. We sat in the garden and she helped me to remember the Cyrillic script by telling me borrowed words such as 'ra-di-o' and 'tak-si', then showing me how they looked. The script came more quickly than I had thought it would; the grammar was another matter. It had all the cases and genders of Latin with none of the logic. Well no, that's not true. It has its own beautiful logic, but not one easily called to mind when you have started a sentence and are in urgent need of a verb. The choice is pock-marked with pit-falls.

I loved it. I loved the sound of it, the complexity of it, the feeling that I was carving out an area of privacy for myself in a life that was beginning to feel too narrow. It was a secret language, a code which could open the door on a world I longed to explore. And Tatisha was an expert teacher; she had been teaching in secondary schools for years. As soon as I had the smallest understanding of the grammar I bought the Oxford Russian Dictionary, the Penguin Short Course, borrowed her 'War and Peace' and off I went.

It took me two years. I read it like a poem, a sentence at a time, slowly dragging the meaning out of it. Sometimes I would recognise the beginning of a verb I knew with an incomprehensible ending; I would trawl through the Short Course until I hit on something similar from which I could deduce that this must be how they make their past participles. When I looked up the nouns – there are a lot of nouns in 'War and Peace' and I had to look up nearly all of them – I tried to associate the words that had the same root. 'Birds' for instance. 'Ptitsa'. Anything that started 'pt' in my dictionary had something to do with birds. Except 'ptomaine' which they'd borrowed anyway. God it was slow. But my lunatic system had one great advantage; anything I learned had a context. There it was in the text, being used. I can still remember where I first found some words. 'Between', for instance. About a third of the way down the page, at the left margin. Where I first learned that 'between' required the instrumental case. Gradually I acquired a nineteenth-century vocabulary. Any reference to coke and a burger would have had me floored. I was at my best when they sat in a drawing-room and talked about love.

Tatisha never spoke to me in Russian. 'We have such interesting conversations in English', she said. But her house was always full of Russians. I never heard bad Russian spoken. Not even mine. Only Tatisha's impeccable Petersburg and that of her numerous friends. They weren't all Russian, of course. The house had always been full to over-crowded since she and her Russian husband and their four young boys moved into it. They had been living in the country and Tatisha longed for a house in London. She told God, with whom she spoke regularly, that if he would give her a house in London she would do anything he asked of her. He gave her the house. On the day after they moved in she received a phone call from her Russian Orthodox priest. He needed a home for a young unmarried girl with a baby, whose parents had thrown her out. Now that she had that large house?.....

When I met her the last of the many, many women and children with whom they had all shared their home was on the point of leaving. There were still caravans in the garden for the overflow.

When my fourth novel was completed, submitted to Heinemann and rejected as unsaleable by the sales manager, among others, I threw myself into my Russian studies to avoid heart-break. I thought it was my best so far. About isolation, ageing and dying. Well I thought it was funny. Not all of it, I admit, but some of it. The eighties, I now console myself, was not a good time for gallows humour.

Slowly the unthinkable thought occupied more and more of my mind. I could not do this any longer. I loved Neil, but I could not live with him. I would shout at Tatisha, who had had more than enough of my problems, 'But I can't leave him'. She was endlessly patient. 'If you can't live with him you'll have to', she pointed out.

I lived with Neil for another sixteen months, making up my mind and then changing it. What finally decided me was the memory of my sister. I hope her daughter Mary and her two sons, my good friends, will forgive me if I say that Vicky had married a difficult man; and stayed with him until she pre-deceased him at fifty-six. Aneurisms were given as the cause of death. I think exhaustion helped. I began to understand that if I stayed with Neil I would go down with him. That there was a life out there I hadn't lived. That it was time to go out and live it. I had promised Neil for all those years that I would never leave him and now I prepared to break that promise.

I told him. Then I phoned all the organisations connected with his welfare. Again. This time I was more forthright. 'I have done your job for twenty-eight years. Now it is your turn. A week from today I will be leaving. My husband will need....'. And I told them. A doctor came to see Neil. Not our G.P., a woman. You know those disgusting little bits of stuff that you sometimes have to pick out of the plug-hole in the kitchen sink? That was exactly the level of disgust with which she regarded me. But I had made up my mind. And in a week's time I left.

XIV

I then wasted three years. In a limbo of guilt and depression. It was probably inevitable, but the years from fifty-eight to sixty-one are not good ones to throw away. Years are getting precious by then. I did try the job-centre. 'Are you really looking for work?' the woman asked me. 'Yes' I said. I was. 'Well you're not very likely to find any, are you'? she said, sympathetic but practical. Nice woman. She was right, too. However, I wouldn't like you to think that I did nothing; though I came close in the first five months. Howard and Eve took me in, looked after me and tolerated me during that awful time. I mean, I was awful; they were wonderful.

So was my housing association, 'Hexagon'. It took them the five months, but they finally found a flat for me with a living-room which would accommodate the Broadwood. Till now it had stayed with Neil in Horniman Drive. Then another problem arose. There was nothing in the bank but an overdraft and my allowance as an unemployed person was not sufficient to move a small suitcase, never mind a grand piano. Even a semi-grand piano. The next tenants of Horniman Drive would be unlikely to welcome a piano of any sort which occupied one quarter of their living room. It would take a specialist removal firm to get it into my first-floor flat, the only access to which is via the eighteen steps of a fire-escape. The outer front-door at the top of it leads into a narrow passage with two inner front-doors. You're faced with an un-navigable right-angle when you open mine. It could only be hauled in through the window.

I don't know whether to be proud or ashamed but I feel obliged to tell you that the Broadwood was moved at the tax-payers' expense. Legless, keyboard upright, with one man operating the block-and-tackle and another holding it away from the house with a rope on the way up, it just made it through the window, whose Victorian panes were hanging on their sash-cords. Then it was re-assembled in the large angular bay, standing on three steel plates, each 2ft. square, placed diagonally in order to reach from joist to joist and prevent its going straight through the ceiling of the flat below.

I thought that another move would finish the pair of us and decided that we should both die here. It was built in 1902 – I have since acquired the letter confirming its provenance – so it is my senior by 24 years. But it is still playable. Just. Still played and loved, as I had promised its only other owner. When I have to leave, at last, I will willingly give it to anyone who will restore it, then play it and love it as much as I have. Before you leap at this offer I should warn you that it is unlikely to cost you less than £10,000. Possibly more. But I thought I'd mention it. Just in case there's another Broadwood fanatic out there.

I could not bear to go back and collect clothes, all the things I should have packed up and brought with me. I made a list and the children did it for me. (They were young adults of 24, 23 and 21, but what should I call them?). I reasoned that if I couldn't remember that I had a thing I couldn't need it. Every now and then I think 'I wonder what happened to that Jesuit china … ?, or some other piece of stuff. But I recommend the method; it simplifies things quite wonderfully.

Neil was still living in Horniman Drive. When I left this time, Matthew moved in. He stayed with his father for a year until Neil found his own solution, in the quiet woman-alone who had been the children's teacher in primary school and who had become a friend to us both in Kent, in the house we had visited together. She wisely built him a studio which stood apart from the house, in which she installed Neil's keyboard and his recording equipment. Or so I am told. We used to call her the blessèd Eileen, but we were genuinely grateful.

You may think – many did – that Matthew stayed with Neil to do what I should have been doing; or that he was making use of rent-free accommodation. I know the reason. He stayed so that I wouldn't go back.

So. I'm fifty-eight and feeling like a woman who has gone out in a dressing-gown to collect the milk and heard the front door slam behind her. Not that I wanted to go back. But I couldn't see any way forward. I had seriously under-estimated the effect of losing what had filled my life for thirty years. Living with Neil. I tried teaching adults to read, chair-caning, woodwork. I forgot the Hungarian Needlepoint. It was said to be relaxing so I gave it a try which resulted in two cushion-covers and far too much time to think.

Acquaintances fell away, leaving the real friends, friends for life. Howard and Eve, of course, John and Jenny Fernald, David Graham… You haven't met David. When the children were small they used to call him the Smarty King. He would bring them boxes of Smarties and they'd implore him to 'do' Parker and Brains for them, the characters he'd created with his voice for 'Thunderbirds'. When Emma married for the second time it was David she asked to stand in for Neil and make the 'father of the bride' speech. And, of course, to 'do' Parker.

The children came to see me often. Lucy brought her flute with her and in the summer, when it was too hot to close the windows, Clare, my new neighbour, heard Lucy playing a Mozart flute concerto while I sketched in the orchestral part. This resulted in the Tuesday evenings we still miss. Clare played both the flute and the violin – later the cello – and was prepared to tolerate my atrocious sight-reading. After a shared bottle of wine with supper at half time there was no stopping us. Tuesday was an oasis in the week, which only came to an end when Clare and her partner Mary moved to Malvern. These occupations floated like becalmed flotsam on a deep depression which nothing would shift. Occasionally Mary, who lectured to psychiatric nurses, would ask if I could possibly lend her some pain-killers.

On one of my numerous visits to talk with Tatisha she said 'Lina Prokoviev's over here now. She's taken a flat in Bryanston Square. You could go and see her if you like. But she's a very difficult woman.' When the pianist Boris Zakharov, Tatisha's father, and Sergei Prokoviev left the Petersburg Conservatoire they remained friends; when they married their children played together. I could go and meet the composer's wife? His first wife? The Princess Lina in 'Love for Three Oranges'? The woman had spent eight years in the gulag; she was entitled to be difficult 'I'd love to,' I said. 'Of course I would.'

A few days later I took my flowers and set out for Bryanston Square. That was the beginning of a friendship that lasted until her death, about three years later. Yes, she could be difficult. We were such an ill-matched pair; she had lived, and was still living in a world of which I knew nothing.   From time to time I'd get it wrong and she would shout 'Ah, you stupid woman!' I'd laugh, and in seconds she'd be saying 'Oh, I didn't mean it, I didn't mean it' and we'd carry on as usual.

Soon I was going to see her every week; doing some shopping for her in Selfridges or going out to lunch with her on her furniture-buying expeditions for the still rather empty flat, - oh, she was such good company. She was a tiny, fierce, obstinate woman; fierce, obstinate and courageous. Qualities which must have enabled her to survive those eight years in the gulag.

By now she was ninety years old. I went to her 90th birthday party in the home of her son Oleg and his wife Frances. Her sight was going by then, but she managed to make a recording of her late husband's 'Peter and the Wolf' by reading from boards the size of a large tray with the text in letters about 4 inches high. I still have the record she gave me.

She was always trying to give me money and that was the one thing I didn't want from her. Finally she said 'Now. You can't refuse this.' She showed me a ring, a square of green malachite set in an anonymous metal. 'It's not worth anything' she said. Well it is to me. All of it.

I still haven't mentioned the thing that kept me going: not just once a week but every day. I know. I've been saving it up, looking forward to writing about it. It was of course, Russian. The language and the literature. When I had finished reading 'War and Peace' Tatisha lent me novels by Goncharov, (what about 'Oblomov'?), Leskov's short stories, all kinds of things I'd never heard of from Russia's golden age, the nineteenth century – my refuge since childhood. Then she tried Pushkin. His long poem, 'The Bronze Horseman', to be precise. That was when I discovered that while reading 'War and Peace' in English had given me something fairly close to the pleasure of reading it in Russian, poetry was another matter. I had never read poetry except when compelled to in order to pass my School Certificate. I read on, stunned. Here was the man who had found Euclid's beautiful straight line, the line I keep searching for. There was this almighty struggle between the state and the individual. (The individual loses). Peter the

Great had been hell-bent on breaking his 'window into Europe', even if it meant building Petersburg on a low-lying swamp subject to floods. I got to the bit where Pushkin writes what I read as a hymn to urban living, the exhilaration of the 'season' in Petersburg. I thought yes, yes. That's why I love London.

I tried to translate that bit. Then I went back to the beginning and translated the whole thing. I re-read that translation for the first time a couple of years ago. It reminded me of a vintage comedian, Ted Ray, Robin's father, who once said that he'd been sent a script that was so bad he had to re-write it before he could tear it up. But it made me realise one important thing. The person who benefits most from any translation is the translator. By the time you have sucked the juice out of every last Russian idea, thrown all the English words into the air which are in any way connected with it, found two that rhyme (sometimes three in Pushkin's case), shunted them along to the end of the line, while attempting to preserve the music of the thing and rejecting anything that Jane Austen could not have said naturally in prose, continually asking yourself 'How would Pushkin have said that if he'd been an Englishman?', you feel as close to the poem as you're likely to get. And to the poet with whom you have now formed a relationship. It is addictive. Somewhere between a crossword and fine art. You'll never stop once you've started. And it has this additional advantage; you can take the weight off your psyche for an hour or two by trying to inhabit someone else's.

Why is Jane Austen my standard? Because both Pushkin and Jane Austen wrote on the cusp of classicism and romanticism, and they took the best from both. Because they express so much in so few words, because they can both write with such wit and such grace that their profundity is sometimes overlooked.

I'm sure you've read Jane Austen. Do you remember when Elizabeth Bennett goes to stay with her friend Charlotte, now Mrs Collins? Austen writes that Charlotte had not yet grown accustomed to her position as the vicar's wife, to her new home, her parishioners, her chickens ... Yet. That 'yet' reveals the pain of an intelligent woman without private means to whom her society offers only two roles;

married woman or governess. 'Yet' looks ahead to a lifetime with a man she knows to be a stupid, pompous crawler. Don't tell me Jane Austen hadn't thought about that 'yet'. She was of an age to be Pushkin's aunt. Their genius is perhaps all they have in common; but they are so alike.

I'm not equally sure you've read Pushkin. You may not know that in 1704 a little Abyssinian boy, ten years old, was abducted, sold into slavery and bought as a present for Peter the Great. Peter really took to the boy. What an intelligent child. He freed him, had him baptised, acting as his godfather, educated him, sent him to Paris to study military matters. On his return he became a successful general and married a Dutch woman who produced a child of the wrong colour. He divorced her and married a German woman. They had ten children whose mixed-race was satisfactorily evident. And in 1799 the little Abyssinian boy's great-grandson was born. Alexandr Sergeevich Pushkin. He was writing poetry as a child, publishing at fifteen... You see? There he was, writing like an angel in Russian, speaking with his parents in French. And there I was, spending an hour or two every day in his company.

An hour or two was not enough. The depression deepened. The arrival of papers concerning divorce proceedings against me contained a description of my heartless behaviour which nearly finished me; I knew that a competent lawyer was doing his job - the lurid language was not Neil's – but he confirmed my own evaluation of the situation. I phoned Sarah, still working at 'Next' in Fenchurch Street. 'Bring the letter and come. Now', she said, loudly and slowly, when she could fit the words in between my sobs. When I arrived at the shop she told her employer that she was going out for a couple of hours and would be back. Then, over coffee, she spent most of those two hours talking me down into sanity. What a woman.

When I got home I sat on the edge of the bed and thought 'Either I end it now, or I do something with this bit of life I've snatched back'. I wasn't contemplating suicide. I was blackmailing myself into action. I picked up the phone and rang the number Tatisha had long since given me, that of SSEES – the School of Slavonic and East European Studies, London University. 'Do you accept mature students'? I asked.

They did. 'Of sixty-two?'. Age was immaterial. 'I'd like to apply for a place on a full-time degree course in Russian language and literature'. They offered just such a course and would send me the necessary information. I put down the phone and poured myself a drink.

XV

SEES was then housed in Senate House, the Stalinesque building on Malet Street. The second and third floors. My fear that I wouldn't find it slightly obscured my anxiety about the forthcoming interview. But I left so much time for getting lost and being late that I ended up spending an hour in a nearby coffee-shop. Then I felt the anxiety. What on earth had I done? I had brought my translation of 'The Bronze Horseman' with me – I was still proud of it – to prove that I had at least made a start.

Professor McMillin could not have been kinder. No one had ever heard of the Matriculation Exemption of fifty years earlier, but it was accepted in place of A levels. I was given the exam paper which the first-year students had just sat and asked to complete it at home in the allotted time; and to submit an essay on the imagery in 'The Bronze Horseman'. I was directed upstairs for an aural test. An aural test. It couldn't get any worse. I must have said something, but I can't recall anything coherent. Then they let me go.

I tried to concentrate on the fact that no one had said no. Yet. I sat at my writing table – the pine trestle-table which Howard had made for us – and worked my way through the exam paper. Then I contemplated writing an essay, another thing I had done fifty years earlier. Novels were one thing. You could make those up as you went along. But an academic essay? What was imagery? Perhaps I didn't really know. I looked it up in the Oxford Dictionary. 'Visually descriptive or figurative language'. Better look up 'figurative', just in case. 'Departing from a literal use of words; metaphorical'. Did you know that 'cladogenesis' means 'the formation of a new group of organisms or higher taxon by evolutionary divergence from an ancestral form'? Don't you just love dictionaries? I resisted the temptation to look up 'taxon', wrote the essay and sent it to SSEES with my attempt at the first-year exam. They let me in. They offered me a place for the following September. Though I would have to start in the second-year. I still regret missing that 'Russian from scratch to A level' first-year course; it would have been the perfect complement to my own chaotic system. I would also have to choose a subsidiary subject for my first two years as I had no previous degree. I chose English literature. What else? They had let me in. Nothing else mattered.

When I was awarded a grant by the London County Council – fees and a living allowance – I realised how lucky I was to be starting in the second year. The grant was for 'four years including one year abroad'; they might not have agreed to that extra year at the outset. In 1987 everyone was entitled to a first degree. I admitted to the interviewer that the LCC had already paid for my four years at the Royal Academy of Music. But all I had to show for it was a gold medal. Or rather, a piece of paper saying that I had been awarded a gold medal, last seen where Milly had placed it, levelling up an uneven bit of floor under the carpet. I couldn't even produce that; but he took my word for it and paid up. I apologise to any student who happens to be reading this. Whoever found it acceptable that young graduates should start their professional lives owing thousands has never been in debt himself. He can't have been.

There followed a happy period of nearly a year, living on the kudos of having got into the university without actually having to do anything. Except, of course, to attend two weddings; Emma's and Sarah's. I'm beginning to feel that I may have been over-cautious in leaving my children to tell their own stories. My life has always been – and is now – so closely connected with theirs.

Emma was first. Hers was a traditional white wedding. The service took place in Magdalen College chapel; Bob and Jill gave her a splendid reception at Woodperry, their great Oxfordshire house. I remember being so happy for her that I couldn't even feel the pain of my reckless shoes. (Heels are really not an option but I'd thought, ah, the hell with it). Emma threw her bouquet and Sarah caught it; this meant, of course, that she too would be married within the year. And she was.

Sarah married in black and white. Her black hat was perfect. And expensive. I went with her to choose it and had to phone Emma to help me persuade her to the extravagance. Emma was painting a room at the time but she downed tools and joined us in central London. She agreed with me that this was an indispensable hat, and together we goaded Sarah into buying it. It was worth it. I have the pictures. Emma's too. And Matthew's and Lucy's. Framed and hanging in the family gallery which is also my bathroom.

Shortly after Sarah's wedding the first day of term arrived; I walked twice round Russell Square and only forced myself to enter the university by considering the shame that would follow if I didn't. The first class – and it was a class, not a lecture – revealed to me that I had made a terrible mistake. I was not going to be able to remember all this. I spent the whole first term either working or sleeping. Not just at night but at any time. I went to visit the children and fell asleep; I fell asleep on a friend's new white sofa with a cup of black coffee in my hand. In those last years with Neil I had frequently fallen asleep on the studio sofa when asked to help put his tapes in order. There was no way of doing this, no system to be uncovered and classified. Sleep, instant and overpowering, was my escape. Now I was falling asleep because I was tired. Gradually my memory ratcheted up, notch by notch, to meet the new demands being made on it. Then, perversely, I lost the knack of sleeping through the night. While starting early in the morning and staying awake all day. But I was keeping up. Somehow. It was exhilarating and I loved it. All of it. The only sadness in that first year was the death of Lina. I went to a funeral service for her in Blackheath, although there was to be something more grand and formal later in Paris. I believe it was Stephen Isserlis who played Prokofiev so beautifully for the occasion.

Weekends would be for essays, either English or Russian. These always started in the same way; jelly-babies for energy and the Oxford dictionary for looking up the key words in the title. And the bible. My godmother had given me a bible when I was confirmed. (There was no choice in the matter of confirmation; we were all done together. The bishop came to the school). I now remembered that this bible had a most valuable asset – a concordance. Another way of looking at those key words.

Oh, I had such fun. You wouldn't believe. Those young people in my year looked only faintly surprised and then accepted me; we were all trying to get through the same amount of work and we'd all chosen the same course. I don't think it was one that appealed to the half-hearted, or someone who really wanted to study engineering but had settled for second-best. Suddenly I was surrounded again by young people, and if I felt – and sometimes behaved – as if I had been given a chance to be young again only this time to enjoy it, I make no apology. That's how it was.

There were classes in grammar, translation, lectures on Russian history, small tutorial groups – sometimes only three or four of us – on Russian literature. It would, of course have been possible to read those novels and plays and poems in English translations. Pointless, but possible. Though if you had just spent a night of passion and were slightly hung-over and there was a life to be had out there I can see that it would save a lot of time. But I had heard someone say that it was the people who read everything in Russian that got firsts. True or not, I wasn't leaving anything to chance. I had found the thing that filled the Neil-sized gap in my life and I was out to make the most of it.

It was at a lecture one Friday afternoon that I first heard of Griboedov, Pushkin's near-contemporary, born four years earlier in 1795. 'There's this wonderful verse comedy by Alexander Griboedov' David Budgen told us. 'But it's completely untranslatable'. Then he read us some excerpts from 'Woe from Wit'. The challenge was irresistible. After the lecture I went to SSEES library, and borrowed the book. I could see the problem. Brevity is the soul of wit and all that but Griboedov had taken this cliché to extremes in a language so condensed, so allusive and so well-directed to those who already knew what he was talking about. Dr Budgen had a point. Still. I tried the speech he had read us...

Towards the end of the year I thought to look at some old first-year examination papers. We were probably advised to do so. It seemed a good idea to try one out; to answer one of the questions in the time that would be available – say, 40 minutes. The attempt resulted in instant despair. This was another skill altogether; no jelly-babies, no Oxford dictionary or bible, no long peaceful weekend. It was a skill I would have to acquire. Fast. I looked at my few panic-stricken sentences leading nowhere and photo-copied a pile of old papers. Then I cut them up into separate questions, put them all in an envelope and picked one out at random. I would answer that question in 40 minutes; even if I knew nothing about the poem and had not read the book. It's amazing what you can deduce from a question; I remembered that Tatisha claimed to have written on the novels of George Sand in her finals at Oxford, knowing only the titles. It had to be possible. At least I would have read the stuff when we got to the real thing. I picked out and answered a question a day, sitting in the library among silent people thinking, which was as close as I could get to the real thing, until we did get to it. It must have helped. I won the Michael Yukhotsky prize for first-years; I didn't even know it was on offer. I began to realise that sixty-two was a very good age at which to go to university. A gap year may be good, a gap of forty-four years is even better. I felt for those young men I used to see slumped over a heap of books in the library, their half-formed, streetwise faces softened in sleep. I think the young women were tougher; but all of them needed to live as well as to study; I only needed to study.

XVI

I have never been one of those grandmothers you hear about; baking treats for after school, giving advice on how to manage parents, bringing confusion to maths homework. Selfless women, earning the enduring affection of their grandchildren. I have eight now and I love them all. And – yet another example of the unfairness of life – their unearned affection is just as great a happiness to me.

My first grandchild was born on 22nd August, 1989. I waited by the phone in a state of acute anxiety which replaced all sensible thought, picked up 'War and Peace', opened it at random and read about the death of the little princess in childbirth. Not for long, of course. Just till I noticed what I was reading. As a portent, this was a failure. Totally inaccurate. Emma gave birth without misadventure to a healthy boy, now a highly intelligent, witty young man with an autistic take on life, who refers scathingly to those of us who lack this as 'neuro-typicals'. Five of my eight grandchildren and one of my daughters are on the autistic spectrum; all of them articulate, complicated people, all of them diagnosed late. I am proud to say that I have a photograph of Robert in early infancy, fast asleep on my shoulder while I read Shakespeare; a rare instance of baby-sitting.

I had chosen Shakespeare for the second year of the English course on the grounds that I would never otherwise read him at all. Just keep meaning to. Only two of us chose Shakespeare, which resulted in a tutorial I still enjoy in retrospect. It came about like this: English at U.C.L. was tomorrow morning; we were to discuss the sonnets; the other young woman had flu; and I had not read the sonnets. I hurtled through them that night as though I were reading a novel. The order of the sonnets is debatable, they are a collection of poems, not an autobiography. I know, I know. Nevertheless, read as I read them for the first time they are a knock-out. I've carried them about in my handbag ever since. There is this exquisite young man. Shakespeare is besotted with him, urges him to reproduce his beauty before it fades.

'For where is she so fair whose uneared womb disdains the tillage of thy husbandry?'

Any virgin would be glad to have him.

'Thou art thy mother's glass, and she in thee calls back the lovely April of her prime' he points out. So what does he do, this beautiful young man? Takes Shakespeare's advice and his mistress.

Ah. The tutorial. I turned up for it, still high on the impact of those sonnets, started warily, giving way before the superior knowledge of this man who, I understood, had written books on them. After a while I forgot about the books and dared to argue a point, even to disagree, though it still felt like the high wire without a net. After an hour-and-a-half he looked at his watch 'I should have been somewhere else half an hour ago' he said. 'I'm afraid we'll have to stop'. Just for a moment – well, an hour-and-a-half – we had no longer been pupil and teacher but two people with a lot of living behind us sharing an equal joy. It's not something that can happen in groups, however small.

I loved the groups, too; and the lectures. All that knowledge and understanding and expertise placed at my disposal. I just had to turn up. Take the bus to Lewisham, the train to Charing Cross, the underground to Goodge Street and walk to Senate House. The journey, as such journeys do, retreated into my sub-conscious; I can still find myself going down on the escalator at Charing Cross, making for the Northern Line, when what I had in mind was the National Gallery in Trafalgar Square. I enjoyed all of it. History, illuminating what I would have missed in the literature. Grammar classes, translating such gems as 'I out-went (on foot, of course; it makes all the difference) with-fifty with-four with-roubles in (my, presumably) in-pocket. A sentence mined with case-endings. Those verbs of motion, designed like a border with armed guards and barbed-wire to keep out foreigners. And the literature ... the solitary pleasure of reading my way through that golden age, the 19th century.

The day was always a sociable affair; noisy and friendly in the canteen at lunchtime, silent in the library until it closed at 7 p.m. Then home to a supper of steak and broccoli, which only takes a minute or two to cook and not much longer to eat. I must have made something else occasionally, and I'm addicted to fruit, but it's the supper I associate with that time of high endeavour and low calories. I expect the jelly-babies helped. I probably munched them as I read after supper, feet up, on the bed. All those 19th century novels and stories. Turgenev (a lot of sitting in drawing-rooms and talking about love in those) Tchekhov's short stories. I'd vaguely thought of Tchekhov as a writer of strange plays mysteriously labelled 'comedies'. But his stories … He said such a good thing about writers: 'The artist's job is not to solve the problem; the artist's job is to state the problem correctly'. Jane Austen would have agreed with him. Like her, over and over again, he states the problem correctly; 'The Archbishop', 'Ward No. 6' ….. I only began to appreciate the plays when I'd read the stories.

And then there was Tolstoy. I lost all patience with Anna Karenina once she'd chosen that unreliable man instead of her son. I should have read it earlier. But 'War and Peace'. Tolstoy showing us before he tells us, so that by the time he breaks cover and comes out with his theory of history, we have already seen it in action. He has his excellent plan – short chapters with one message. It lent itself admirably to my colour-coded 'Find a quote in "War and Peace"'. Some Hero of the Soviet Union had summarised every chapter in Tatisha's edition; I borrowed it back, photo-copied the forty pages of summaries and had endless fun high-lighting all the names – gold for Pierre, green for those nasty Kuragins, pink for the Rostovs; then drawing red squiggly lines beside each chapter-summary to indicate 'War' and blue straight ones for 'Peace'. Et cetera. Gold with green characters flanked by straight blue lines will find you Pierre and Helene in a non-military setting. I have been phoned by Russians in search of a particular scene.

Oh, Tolstoy. I can't accept his historical theories and I don't admire his behaviour, but if you want to know how a young girl feels as she leans from a window on a summer's night, he is your man. As his wife wrote in her diaries, 'If only he would show me one iota of the understanding he devotes to his characters …' As for his views on the ideal marriage …

'If all were minded so, the times should cease, and threescore year would make the world away'. As Shakespeare wrote in support of the opposite policy. Though even he did not envisage more children for his beautiful young man.

'Ten times thyself were happier than thou art, If ten of thine ten times refigured thee'; Tolstoy's eleventh was born as 'The Kreutzer Sonata' was published – he never could align the warring sides of his nature, poor man. He made rules for himself, he studied assiduously, but his diary as an eighteen-year-old shows him already torn in two. After planning a day of strenuous self-improvement which would have floored the most devoted academic, he writes: 'After supper, rules - or the gypsies.'

Then there was Leskov. Sometimes writing as a Russian Orthodox Trollope, sometimes making a study of simple greed and brutality in 'Lady Macbeth of Mtsensk, the story which inspired the opera.

I'd better stop. But you get the picture. I am enjoying myself like never before. I may, just possibly, have over-done it. By the end of the second year I had become anxious. I went to see the university doctor, an extremely understanding woman who had seen it all before. She gave me some beta blockers to get me through the end of year exams. Either I had an unpredictably strong reaction to them or – more likely – I had absent-mindedly taken the recommended dose twice. I arrived late for the first exam and met the invigilator looking for me as I sauntered down the corridor to where it was all happening. He showed me to my table; I sat down, folded my arms on it and laid my head on them. Out of the corner of one eye I noticed a sheet of paper covered with questions. Ah. Yes. I sat up slowly and started to answer them. Say what you like, I was relaxed.

The really important thing that took place that summer was the competitive interview for a chance to spend ten months in what was still, in 1990, the Soviet Union. I wanted a place on that course. I wanted to see where the Rostovs would have lived in Moscow (pink for Rostovs), where 'The Seagull' had its first performance at the Moscow Arts Theatre … I hadn't been out of the country for nearly forty years and I wanted an adventure. But I could see that the moment they set eyes on me they would be thinking about insurance and air-ambulances. I only remember the first question: 'What would you do if you were sharing a room with two Russian girls who'd never heard of Pushkin and talked endlessly about their boyfriends, and a homesick English student who did nothing but cry?' I said 'What a marvellous plot for a novel. I'd make notes'. Fortunately they laughed. More importantly, they gave me a place. In Moscow, what's more. Half of the students went to Voronezh. I expect the air-ambulance would have been cheaper from Moscow.

We were given a sheaf of advice which I'm sure would have worried my parents if I'd still had any. Try to avoid any medical treatment involving needles – take your own in case. Buy numerous small gifts to ease any transactions which may be necessary. Try to avoid dentistry altogether. Plus, of course, warnings about the more obvious hazards that the young might be more likely to encounter.

My aids test caused hilarity in the London surgery. But at that time everyone arriving in the Soviet Union ran the risk of being tested for aids unless they had a certificate which proved this to be unnecessary. (See 'needles', above). I bought the gifts, hoped to avoid the dentistry and stocked up on dried foods in case of shortages, as advised; lentils, onions, peppers, chicken-stock cubes, milk, even Complan (it makes excellent chicken soup with a stock-cube). And vitamin tablets of various sorts. Then I began to think about the winter – our ten months covered September '90 to June '91. The animal rights movement was powerfully present at that time; there were only three furriers in the Yellow Pages. I phoned the first one. 'Do you sell fur coats'? I asked. 'Why d'you want to know'? he snapped back at me. 'Well I'd rather thought of buying one' I told him. He was instantly apologetic; he explained about the constant hostile phone calls and made me an appointment.

He had gone to ground in a basement and was selling all that remained of his stock – two rails of coats. The ones for women were sheepskin, heavily embroidered. I couldn't do it. However intense the Moscow frosts. Sarah, who had come with me, suggested the men's rail. They were extremely heavy, but more sober altogether. I bought a double-breasted one in dark brown beaver-lamb, with a low half belt in the same fur. It looked – and was – impenetrable. I wasn't certain how far I'd be able to walk in it without needing to sit down. But no frost could touch it.

The summer raced towards autumn. On 8th September all four children accompanied me to Heathrow and joined the group of proud parents. I took one last look at them as I dragged my luggage towards the point of no return, thought about my inability to find my way in London where I had lived all my life and wondered if I would ever see them again. They tell me that they wondered too.

XVII

Before I left for Moscow I told the children that I would write one letter for all four of them; I asked them to pass these letters round and then save them for me. And they did. I put them in a folder on my return and forgot about them. When I finished Chapter 16 I thought I would just look at them in case there was anything I'd forgotten. I couldn't find them. They had been on a bookshelf in the same brownish folder for twenty three years. They must be there. They weren't. Interest sharpened into need. Had they been victims of my ruthless throw-out policy? I had never yet regretted anything I'd chucked; this could be a first. I searched the sensible places. Then I tried the wardrobe, the airing-cupboard and the chest of drawers. It's a very small flat. There wasn't anywhere else. I phoned Emma. Were they with the family photographs? They were not. As a last throw I tried logic and pulled out the box-file at the bottom of the heap, labelled 'Prose'. Well. They weren't poetry. And there they all were, pages and pages of thin A4 airmail paper, closely written on both sides. I put my feet up, started to read and experienced such a rush of nostalgia that I had to get the vodka and the little salted cucumbers out of my Catford fridge and toast my sixty-four-year-old self. As I blundered through this alien culture, suddenly deprived of the power of speech, sounding like a grateful idiot. 'Thank you'. 'It is very good'. 'I like it'. Even, in extreme cases, 'I like it very much'.

I lasted about a week like this, hardly daring to speak in case I got it wrong. Then I thought – I'm here for ten months. If I don't communicate with Russians I shall die. The hell with mistakes. I opened my mouth and said anything. If I couldn't think how to say what I wanted to say I said something else. I can only hope that most of it was incomprehensible ...

I have persuaded myself back to the present with great difficulty and decided to quote from the letters. If you find their persistent cheerfulness wearing, do remember - I was writing to my children.

What was I going to do, terrify them? I admit, I have wept unreasonably in Marina's kitchen over the Russianness of Russians. (You will meet Marina.) Nevertheless. Now that I've found them I can't bear to waste them. So here are some of the first, euphoric paragraphs of my letters from the Soviet Union in the September of 1990.

'Moscow!!!

Hello darlings! (To anyone who doesn't qualify and reads this, it's a letter to my family, not a travelogue).

Now. I love it. Even the awful bits are satisfyingly predictable. I've stood on the stage of the Moscow Arts Theatre. I've queued for black bread and seen the onion domes in Red Square in brilliant autumn sunshine. I'm here, I'm here, I'm really here. I came back from Red Square on the metro. On my own. And didn't get lost. I am at this very minute cooking the lentils which stood so long on my chest of drawers, because there doesn't seem to be anything else to eat, and I am very, very happy'. I was too. And I would like to point out that my lentil soup, cooked with the dried onions, peppers, herbs, tomato puree and chicken stock cubes I had brought with me was not so much a soup; more of a life-support system. Back to the letters.

'We started late and arrived at 4ish, Moscow time. We were shouted at for jumping the queue (somebody knew a man) and then had to wait till 7p.m. because some of the luggage had been put on the wrong flight.... At 8.30 p.m. we arrived at the Moscow University Hotel. Very pleasant. Just one problem. They didn't have any rooms booked for us'. They had, of course, but they had managed not to know this. 'We sat on our suitcases in the foyer. That's when I met Dafydd. We chanced to sit on adjacent suitcases, talked about the only thing we had in common – our love of Russian literature – and began what was to be a lifelong friendship. It seems unnecessary to say that he was Welsh. He was also painfully clever and very good company. Everyone argued about us.... By midnight they agreed that we could sleep on the floor in the rooms of the Voronezh contingent who'd arrived the day before. Slept like a log ... At 8.45 a.m. we gathered as instructed in the foyer. We sat on the cases ... Cabbage, black coffee and mineral water in the buffet. We sat on the cases. The embassy has been alerted. They are not best pleased. Letters will be sent. Justine, our 'group-leader', is pulling out every stop. The Voronezh contingent leave. Suddenly and unexpectedly. Half of them are out seeing the sights and are due for a nasty shock on their return. This must be so that we can have their rooms, we think. Wrong. Just as the buffet is about to open again a very old bus arrives, the luggage is piled in and we are taken to the hostel in North-east Moscow which Justine, on our behalf, has been fighting to avoid.

At 5 p.m. we arrive at the hostel. We sit on the suitcases. A sweepstake is organised on the time that the first actual bed is sighted. At 6.15 p.m. Louise wins 75 roubles and I get the bed, which I prefer to 75 roubles or indeed to any other amount you care to name'.

Unlike the university's hotel, this hostel provided no food; there was a communal kitchen with a cooker, a row of sinks and a fridge. 'Caviar and black bread for breakfast. Justine is off to the Embassy. The big question is – will we move today? (Back to the hotel). Or tomorrow? Or some other time instead? ... The group is knocking on our door at 10 a.m. and we are going out somewhere to have breakfast (Justine's duty-free caviar being just a preliminary snack, you understand) ... To Pushkin Square at 7 p.m. to find the Stanislavskii Theatre. All 20 of us are seeing a Leskov play. Then who knows? Oh yes. There's a meeting. In our room'. I was sharing with Justine which was just as well. We laughed so much and so helplessly at so many things that could otherwise have been disasters. 'More duty-free and caviar. Well. You can't let it go to waste. At the moment it's trapped in a plastic bag on the window ledge (the communal fridge imparts a flavour all its own) with the open ends dangling inwards. We are five floors up. Ingenious, huh? I see it like camping but indoors'.

I had not been out of the country for nearly forty years. Here I was no one's daughter, no one's wife, no one's mother; here no one knew more of me than they saw or heard. Surely I couldn't have another fresh start? I could, though. Once I had dragged my knowledge of 19th century Russian off the paper and related it to the unknown language I heard all around me. Temporary problems could be regarded as an entertainment – it was the sort with no solution I was worrying about. What if I never understood spoken Russian? The anxiety engendered by this thought slowed down the learning process considerably.

The second letter begins: 'I can't believe I've only been here since Thursday ... Let me tell you about the metro. It's great. Palatial – they were to be the people's palaces – clean, no graffiti, fast (as are the escalators) and frequent.

10.30 a.m. An heroic babushka is cleaning the lavatories. Give this woman a medal. She is, of course, merely reducing them to a state where questions would be asked in the house ... Personally I think she should have left it to fossilize. The pungent ammoniac smell of disturbed excrement is head-spinning. The hotel floats like a mirage before us. Friday, perhaps? Or next week?

10.45. Eight of us travel by the blessed metro to the centre of Moscow and find a wonderful place for breakfast. Tea (black, of course) and the most delicious soft white rolls filled with mushrooms and onions before baking. Bozhe moi!' O M G now seems to be the equivalent exclamation.

'4.30. The same seven invite me to join them. Someone has found a private restaurant near Pushkin Square. We eat in stifling heat and near total darkness (it is sunny outside), meat dumplings in broth and ice-cream with nuts. By this time I have a roaring cold and am hell-bent on not missing anything.

7 p.m. The Stanislavskii Theatre. I fall asleep, miss the beginning and only slowly gather a thread or two of this Leskov story. It's about a serf theatre, a wig-maker and a brutal serf-owner. It breaks frequently into deeply sentimental music – singing and dancing – with dreams about an orthodox wedding, crowns held over the heads of the star-crossed lovers, and what with the heat and the good food and my cold I gradually give in to it and mourn for the bad old days with the best of them. I think the Soviets are going through their Laura Ashley phase.

I have just had a blinding revelation. Russians can dance in a sitting position because they develop incredibly strong thigh muscles performing over – but not on – seatless loos.

The Pizza Hut opened today. I've just heard it on the Moscow news.

Competition between them and McDonalds seems to be causing detached amusement ... The McD queue stretches all round Pushkin Square.

First day at the Maurice Torez Institute where we're studying. The hitch in our being given our rooms at the hotel seems linked to the fact that we are not bringing hard currency in but exchanging with Russian students. Guess how we got there? Justine and I overslept, dressed at speed, dashed to the main road and flagged down a car. Not a taxi. Just any old car. Anyone who would stop. (This is common practice). The roads are a menace. So wide, many of them, that I can barely see the green man without my glasses. Of course, you can get half way. Fine till you realise that trams come down the middle. I've had to run for it once or twice. Don't worry. That was before I spotted the green man.'

We filled in a form on our first day. I said that I was a writer. As I was sure of the spelling. This was a most fortunate answer; it led to my enduring friendship with Marina, Professor of Translation. She had just translated 'Lady Chatterley' and needed to proof-read it, but Detgiz (Children's State Publisher) were insisting that she translate traditional Russian fairy-tales for them into English. This is such an unnatural way round; it is customary to translate into one's native language. She took me home to her flat where we sat in her kitchen and pursued our respective trades in a beautiful translators' silence, broken only by my requests for help with an idiom in one of the fairy-tales.

Someone had seen Solzhenytsin on sale outside Shabolovskaia metro. Success! Bought Zamiatin and Vasilii Grossman. Then one copy of 'The First Circle' appeared on the stall. Someone grabbed it. I asked the man if he had any more where that came from. 'Follow me'. I did. A bit. Then said very suspiciously 'Have you got it or not?' Oh god oh god. He led me to another book stall and produced it from a suitcase. I am deeply apologetic.

Our situation is clarifying. A change in the law means that from Aug: 28th the hotel requires 800 roubles a night from us. We have a contract. But not, it seems, to stay in any particular hotel. We hope our contract specifies 'hotel'. If not the first circle is receding. I wouldn't care. It's worth the chaotic living conditions to be here, in the middle

of things, at such an exciting moment. Really there is no point in complaining and insisting. We are a very small part of an enormous economic problem. The west keeps urging the S.U. to 'join the market'. So they are. At our expense, as it happens. The joke is definitely on us.
......

I bought apples from a woman in an underpass. I've just soaked them in Milton, saved the whole ones and cooked the rest. We had them for supper with the last of the Smetana. Plus a tin of meat and Smash from the embassy shop. Delicious. The well balanced diet ...'

The embassy shop – the commissariat, I think they called it – actually was that corner of a foreign field which is forever England. Behind the splendid building overlooking Moscow River, in what may have once been stables, upholding the entertaining culture, it sold the stuff your Hampstead hostess might require. The only concession to abroad were the plastic vodka glasses. Then there were comfort foods for the nostalgic; rich tea biscuits, milk chocolate and marmalade, plus fish-fingers, marmite and tomato sauce for the children. We were privileged to spend £30 a month there in view of the current shortages, with certain restrictions – only one small bar of chocolate, for instance. It was a wise precaution. The twenty of us could have cleaned them out.

'The central heating is on! I don't have to sleep in a nightdress, a thermal vest and a sweater under three blankets. On the other hand the cockroaches are out in force. I've killed two on the bed and one on this letter. Well – I shook it off first. Promise.' I didn't tell them about the enamel washing-up bowl I took from a pile in the kitchen. I uncovered a seething black layer of cockroaches which I washed off in one of the sinks, glancing down first to make sure it was connected to a drain. Not all of them were. Or that when a sink was blocked and the overflow poured into the corridor instead of unblocking it planks were laid down in the corridor ...

But the theatre... 'The play went on for four hours. I am developing overdoing it into an art-form. Came back (with Pete for escort) on the metro. In by midnight. Very loud party on the fifth floor corridor. (Ours). Quite a striking flood tonight.' I must have told them about the flood. 'Grated carrot, I think, blocking one of the sinks. Inches deep in the corridor. Someone being sick on the landing. Ah! Youth! Bed by 1 a.m. The party is in full swing. Asian pop-music, loud enough, as William Saroyan once said, to make a sensitive schoolgirl giggle. I turn out the light and sleep the deep resting sleep of a baby. Till 8 o'clock in the morning. (Barring one water-logged visit to the loo – half asleep, I'd put on ordinary slippers and got soaked.)

"This is the righte lyfe that I am inne, To flemen alle manner vyce and synne."

As dear Geoffrey would have said if he'd tried the hostel. On second thoughts, condition for his pilgrims were probably remarkably similar. (I take 'flemen' to mean flee, not experience, in case you're worried.)' I checked. It means "banish".

I'm sure that if I had not found the letters I could have given you a sober account of the whole ten months in a short chapter. Now I'm finding it difficult. I had forgotten so much. I had forgotten how it felt not to know that the Soviet Union was about to collapse. Everyone knew something was about to happen. But what? And when? Up above, no doubt, there were vast fortunes being made, villainy of every sort; down below, where I was, Russians were fully occupied in surviving. I was an outsider, sometimes angry, sometimes in despair, but knowing, nevertheless, that I was only there for ten months. As our lecturer said one morning to a depressed looking student 'Cheer up. You can go home. We have to stay here'.

'Something has to happen' I wrote. 'Of course there are the markets; but the time and effort expended because someone has heard there are melons at some metro or other is unbalanced. Out of proportion. Old ladies are selling flowers in twos and threes on the steps down into the metro. Or apples. Anything. A little crowd forms. What have they got? Pink and green creamy cakes covered in nuts. They sell them in boxes that resemble a really good effort by the intake class for mothers' day. Moscow looks as though it is being run by children who have been left to manage for themselves. And in the middle of it all people are living their complicated, sophisticated lives. The Bolshoi season has begun; Moscow Arts Theatre starts soon; we shall watch brilliant talented people playing Chekhov. This morning, outside the Intourist Hotel, Dafydd had to detach, forcibly, a beggar child who had her arms and legs locked around Theresa's leg. We'd given her kopeks, but she kept calling 'rouble, rouble', and hung on. This was a well-trained child.'

Most of the students were still attending the classes. Towards the end of our course Dafydd and I were frequently the only students to turn up. Perhaps we were just greedy. We wanted all of it; Russian language and culture from the academic point of view and what was going on outside the window.

'This morning – (Thursday) – one and a half hour lecture on 18th century Russian literature. This bloke didn't believe in me. "But at home you're a teacher?" he said. Confidently. "No. I'm a student." "But..." (no one is a student at 64) "And I'm a writer." "Aaaah!" He understands. I'm not really a student. Just pretending.'

After a grammar lesson three of us wander by metro and on foot all over Moscow... Dafydd buys a fur hat with ear flaps. The shop is an experience. As if you'd accidentally joined the army and were being issued with hat, one, Muscovite, for the use of. A long counter. One beautiful heavily-made-up assistant who despises everybody. She's the quartermaster. One small mirror – at the head of the queue. Behind the counter a mass of fur hats in pigeon holes. You don't like it? She bangs down another and snatches away the first one. Nobody protests. You like it? She snatches away the one you like and gives you a ticket. You pay at the cash-desk. Then collect. A bit like Foyle's, come to think of it.' But not a lot, I feel obliged to add.

Afterwards, coffee at the Intourist hotel. 'You are supposed to show your hotel card' (to one of the thugs at the entrance with muscles too big for their buttoned-up suits) 'but I do my "Now young man, mind your manners" act' (see cover) 'and the others follow me in. Then we fall on the loos with ecstatic cries and enjoy this rare luxury – the seat.

It can't only be last Thursday... It is though.

Monday. Lecture on all aspects of Soviet Union. Couldn't quite believe my ears. "We're changing the structure of the course. We don't teach Marxist/Leninist philosophy now. Just political philosophy and economics" or words to that effect. It's hard for older teachers who have spent 40 years or more on one track and have suddenly to change direction ... I've just heard some politician on the radio say "We've got to look reality in the face. We have to cut back on arms, etcetera...". Our lecturer promises to take us quickly through the background to the present situation (we reached 1936 in the first lecture.)

Worked in the reading hall at the Maurice Torez. Then to the Cultural Attaché's home. Oh god, glasses of wine or beer and delicate canapés. I'm enjoying myself but the boys had hoped for hefty sandwiches. They fall on the canapés like locusts. The poor man orders sandwiches. When they come it's like offering chocolate biscuits at a children's birthday party. You could, as I always said, lose an arm.

'...went to the Intourist hotel. For the usual reason. Then the one dollar coffee. Pretending that we are not food-obsessed hunter-gatherers. "Hard currency only" the notice said. I don't do this often. It's a horrible feeling. Being privileged in an underprivileged country – as though their rotten notice read "whites only".

The double standard for money is extraordinary. Officially it's ten roubles to the pound. So my lunch at the Maurice Torez cost less than 5p. A complete Tolstoy at 100 roubles is either £10 or half someone's monthly salary. (200 roubles a month is quite common.) What happens when they 'join the market' is a mystery to me. And, I suspect, to a lot of other people...

I shall take my courage in both hands and have a shower. Always providing that no one has mistaken it for the lavatory again. The shower is a steaming hell-hole in the basement. Water – hot, beautiful water-pours unregarded from the pipes, the walls, the ceiling. The floor is awash. Make sure there's a rose on the outlet. You may be hit with a sudden gush straight from the pipe. Nobody turns off taps. Or cookers. Everyone's electricity is no one's electricity. I am doing my best for the Soviet economy by personally turning off every tap I see running. Today I even disconnected the cooker in the kitchen. The switches on the stoves don't work, so the only way to turn them off is to pull a hefty plug on a thick black cable out of the wall. Nobody does. (Except me.) The heat is appalling in there; and the waste hurts my thrifty soul.

You'll probably get all these letters out of sequence. But that could hardly be more confusing than the letters themselves. It's just that I don't want to forget any of this. I shall be glad I came for the rest of my life.' ... I am.

'Another lecture on 18th/19th century literature from this gentle young man in a cardy. He forgot the English for decanter so I told him. I don't know possessed me, but I gave him the most enormous wink. I must have been feeling extra cheerful. Anyway – when it came to a stirring poem by Derzhavin he read the Russian (shaken but not stirred) and asked me to read the English translation to this hall-full of students. I let them have it. In a passionate contralto. "Arise, arise" and a lot more of the same. Well. It was no good doing it in mouse-like English style. The young American next to me looked positively grateful. He said it was the first thing he'd understood all morning. Ah, there is just no end to the amusements here.

Phonetics. Indescribable. I wish you could hear us. We are practising using the back of the tongue. Even those without hangovers soon feel sick.'

This letter ends: 'Goodnight my darlings - look after yourselves. I'm relying on some of us to be sensible.' On to the next one.

'There's no point in killing cockroaches. After all, they got here first. I flick off the ones that are foolish enough to walk onto the stove while I'm cooking. I mean. They could burn their poor little feet.'

Efforts were still being made to deliver us from the hostel. And not just by the embassy. 'Russians are offering their homes to us, complete strangers, people from the Maurice Torez, friends of friends. An old man came to my aid the other day while I was consulting my metro map. Explained a rather tricky change, smiling with pleasure because he'd found someone even more helpless than himself. No smiling once they're in uniform. I'll get a smile out of one of those women who look at my season ticket every day if it takes me the whole ten months.' I didn't. 'I think it's the uniform. I bet that little old man never smiled in uniform. They look as though they are personally responsible for the entire Soviet Union. Perhaps they are.'

A pattern was beginning to emerge; the course, looking for food, a passion for theatre. But there was so much I didn't understand. The evening that reduced me to tears in Marina's kitchen, for instance. I had met Katia and her parents in London when they visited her there. They gave me their phone number and said that I must visit them when I came to Moscow. I phoned when I did, over and over again, without success. Turning up seemed the only solution and Katia had given me their address. I found their flat and they welcomed me warmly, looking stunned. But they fed me tea and apple-cake in their kitchen and suggested a date for a longer visit. As they were just going out. 'Come and have a meal', they said. I found their flat again and presented my red carnations, the ones that were sold from glass fronted boxes outside the metros, warmed against the frost by little candles. Would I mind sitting with Katia's grandmother for a moment? Of course not. I sat on the bed in her room and we chatted. After about twenty minutes they looked in and said that they had to go out now. And left.

Now I can laugh at myself and think of reasons. They had enough to worry about without some demanding, time-consuming foreigner. And then they had been born into the time of the knock on the door in the night, the arrests, the gulag. For no better reason than associating with such a person. Perestroika was, after all, only a word.

At the time it hurt, and I retreated to Marina's kitchen, where everything may be discussed. And then Alla, another Russian girl I had met in London before I left for Moscow, sent me such a funny friendly letter. 'She paid me the nicest compliment' I told the children, 'I shall copy it exactly. "In the first time you'll be hard in USSR. But you are the such men that you'll be have a lot of good friends." How right she is about the friends. Come to think of it, I was a bit hard in the first time, too.'

That was meant to be the end of the chapter. I stopped for a coffee, switched on Radio 3, and someone had just started playing the first movement of Brahms' 1st Piano Concerto. I listened to it with the tears pouring down my face and I am here to tell you that apart from all the other wonderful things that have happened in my life it was worth being born just to play that. I've knocked back a vodka to stem the flow. Perhaps you can tell.

XVIII

After three weeks the problem concerning our accommodation was solved.

'No classes this morning. We're packing up and moving to the Pushkin Institute. Some of the others are very fed up. They should never had seen the university hotel. Five of us sharing one bathroom and loo. With seat. What do they want, blood?

They said the bus would come at three. And we believed them. (When will we learn?) At three we brought down our suitcases. And there we sat. Justine phoned Gosobrazovanoe from time to time. (Min. of.Ed.) They maintained that the bus was there. Waiting for us. It had been ordered. It must be there. A kind of notional bus. A philosophical abstraction. (Perhaps we couldn't see it for the rain.) At 5 o'clock the man from the Maurice Torez went out and waved down a bus. Just any old bus. He offered the driver 50 roubles to take us. The driver wanted a hundred. After much discussion we agreed on the 100 and started loading up the luggage. The real bus turned up. Justine said he should have accepted the 50 and the boys started unloading the luggage. He accepted 10 and gave back the 90. We loaded up the real bus. Somewhere in Moscow there must be one very angry bus queue. You think, perhaps, I am making this up? Or exaggerating? I promise. This is a blow-by-blow account of our afternoon.

We arrived at the Pushkin Institute. Beautiful. Spacious, light, clean-smelling foyer with bronze of Pushkin. Bedrooms are allocated. The same feeling for the proprieties that makes Natalia Ivanovna, our grammar teacher, insist on calling me Meri Ernestovna (the equivalent of Mrs Hobson) came over the uniformed woman allocating them. I should have a single room. But there wasn't one. Would I mind sharing with a Soviet lady? The others are all together in fives and speaking English. I jumped at the chance.' Irina was not only a Soviet lady, 32 to my 64, but a teacher of Russian to the 'equal-rights' republics who came to Irkutsk university and brushed up their Russian before starting on their chosen subjects.

I laughed with Irina nearly as much as I had with Justine. She used to call me a 'hooliganka' because I sometimes used words – the Russian for 'prick', for instance – which no Soviet lady would have uttered. They didn't appear in respectable 19th century novels, but I'd only just learned them and they didn't yet feel unsayable in polite society. That takes time. (The word for prick is 'hooey', and comes loaded with visions of Russian immigrants arriving at Ellis Island. For me, at any rate.)

Bob, whose design group was building or restoring hotels and casinos all over the place, had his eye on an old palace in Granovskaia St., then being used for storing archive material. He was to come to Moscow at some point during my stay and his interpreter was to be Victor Pogostin. I had already met Victor and Natasha and their ten-year-old son. 'Progress Publishing (for whom he's translated some Hemingway) want him to do literal line-by-line translation of poems by a woman from one of the southern republics. If, of course, he knew someone who could make them into poems, so much the better. He suggested me. If all goes well, we'll work on them together. 500 roubles each... Real work! I'm thrilled to pieces!' I didn't meet the poet – Victor arranged everything. I only knew that Umut Kemel'bekova was from Kazakhstan, lived in Moscow and wrote in Russian. I did enjoy her poems. They were so different from anything I had read; filled with a sense of a culture utterly unknown to me. A new element in the pattern emerged. To studying, food-finding and theatre I added thinking about translating. Specially translating poetry. It's a game like no other. A balancing act, a juggling with meaning and music. (It's addictive, too, but I didn't know that then).

Studying still filled the mornings – well – for most of us. 'Let me tell you about today. Our lecturer abandoned his pre-planned schedule and explained the 500 day plan of Shatalin.' Or Shatalin's 500 day plan, as we English say. Russian constructions were evidently seeping into my native language. 'Next week he's going to tell us about Abalkin's. The economy staggers. Victor went today to one of the best delicatessens in Moscow. It was empty. Literally. Nothing to sell. Four assistants doing nothing. I met him at the Peking Hotel; he borrowed my 'in-case-bag', or plastic carrier, and tried the hotel buffet. He came out looking all happy. He'd managed to buy about a kilo of cold fried fish. We had some for lunch. Then we worked on the poems..... Victor is trying to arrange contracts and an advance. You see what a 'biznismyen' I am becoming. While I was there someone phoned to know if I'd give English conversation classes. 100 roubles an hour. 2 hours a week – I'll do it if I can fit it in.' I couldn't.

'Jackson's English Breakfast is holding out well. (But I see my resolve to give away my coffee weakening.) Two x 1-1/2 hour classes of solid Russian this morning, then I'll have lunch in the Institute's 'bufyet'. For which thank God. I bought three apples there yesterday. They sell odd things from time to time. I think the young men find it hardest. They buy bread-rolls or buns, 5 or 6 at a time. Or – in desperation – queue for a Big Mac. I hate to think I even smiled at Muscovites buying bags full of them and taking them home to their families...'

I'm finding it so hard to leave out anything. I've just spent twenty minutes trying not to quote yet another visit to the supermarket. Every time I pick up these letters I stare at the blank page in front of me thinking 'but I've got to tell them that'. I'll omit the empty shelves and the queue that took 25 minutes and just give you one detail. From the little heaps of a few things disappearing rapidly the woman in front of me in the queue for the check-out had taken two chunks of salami. 'I like an optimist. The girl told her "one only – unless this lady .....?" meaning me. I'm getting quicker at this. I bought one of her chunks and then sold it back to her. The girl didn't mind. She helped find the right change ... Then translating with Marina. Marina is the Moscow Tatisha. What a lovely lady. Minute flat, full of books. Full of everything, come to think of it. Restful chaos. Her mind (like yours, Tatisha, if you read this) is definitely on higher things..... we talked about the art of translation, food, Pushkin, families. She fed me borsch and frankfurters and potatoes (I am becoming food-fixated.) We had this wonderful afternoon. Then a bus back to the Pushkin with the shopping, dumped the grapes I'd bought in the street in Milton and off to the Arts Theatre' – the original one that Chekhov saved with his

'Seagull'. After the restoration in the eighties it still flies as an elegant logo above the proscenium arch. 'Now this was the real thing. Sergei Iurskii's wife, Natalia Teniakova, played Ranevskaia brilliantly. A modern woman. Smoking. Running those cheap parties in the ruins. Disillusioned. She'd already lost everything and knew it. Parting with the cherry orchard was only the 'making public' of what everyone knew privately. Not merely time to move on. They already had. The old world appeared from time to time through lit gauzes. Sounds tasteless but I thought it worked. Fiers, the aged retainer, stood like a crumbling monument throughout the play and ended by lying back in an armchair and pulling a dustsheet over himself. Fortunately they had some bread and cheese on sale in the bufyet. And – spectacular – a slice of chocolate swiss-roll. I was beginning to feel really peculiar but the cheese just saved me. It gave me that last spurt of energy needed to be introduced to Natalia Teniakova (She's lovely. It's the Russian). Everything requires to be done in Russian.' Well, yes ...

'Yesterday was another killer. Up at 6 to get to class by 8. What is this? Some kind of initiation ceremony? Glorious morning. Dazzling sun at last. And a degree or two of frost has whitened the grass and hardened the mud. Got to Maurice Torez to find 3 x 1-1/2 hour lessons on the timetable. Finishing at one. That did it. We withdrew our labour. None of us went to the third class. From each according to his capacity, as they say.

I went to Marina's instead. Worked on another fairy-tale... exactly what I love doing. Cutting down, simplifying, until the thing has that rhythmic repetitive hypnotic sound that a story about magic ought to have.

Left at 4 for the Kremlin. Nina's daughter Ol'ga had given me her precious ticket to see the 'Almazny fond' – mmm ... diamond reserves ... Into this marble lined fortress through a door like a bank vault's, to the beautifully mounted exhibition. We started with industrial diamonds. Then we moved into the real stuff. The lights dimmed. The brightly-lit cases were lined totally in black velvet. Breathtaking. Literally. I felt my own indrawn breath, heard everyone else's. Enormous stones. Huge diamonds like stage props. I struggled to believe that these were the real thing.

Oh joy! I have – at the moment – a totally free weekend. Only one party, on Sunday evening. In Justine's room …

I am going to loaf about all morning. I admit to having slightly overdone it .. I shall lie here until my ankles resume their normal size. Then I thought I'd wander down to the Arbat and see if I can find any interesting books. Dafydd tried to buy a teapot yesterday. He heard of a place where they'd been seen. No luck. The man told him "There aren't any teapots and there aren't going to be any teapots." OK, OK. Just so long as we know.'

I think it was G.K. Chesterton who said 'When people stop believing in God they don't believe in nothing; they believe in anything.' Even in 1990 diversity was making a comeback in Moscow. 'Went to Red Square with Irina. It was an Orthodox feast-day and they were having – for the first time in 70 years I think – a service at St. Basils. You know. The psychedelic onion-domes. We couldn't get in. It was, we discovered, by invitation only. We stood in the crowd and watched bearded priests come out carrying censers and plastic 'in-case' bags. In case they spotted any food on the way back to the monastery, presumably. While behind us the Other Lot filed in a steady stream past Lenin's tomb.'

Then there was Sasha and the birch-wood. 'One of our teachers invited us to meet her friends. About 5 of us went. They were – as we had suspected – straight out of the sixties. A sculptor and his wife, an artist, a chemist, a student; they live in the middle of a birch-wood on the edge of Moscow. Barefoot intellectuals, pursuing the healthy life, disciples of some bearded prophet called Ivanov who had just died – in remarkably good health – at the age of 83. Oh, I shouldn't laugh. They were so kind. They made us apple-cake and cheese-cake, glasses of tea, sweets. One of them played the guitar and sang. The walls were lined with birch bark, the little house itself is all of birch, built by the sculptor. The wood was full of rather down-cast mother figures he'd carved. The loo was a triangular hut – a tall thin isosceles – over a hole. We were given photographs of the guru and his rules. They throw buckets of cold water at each other. All through the winter. And swim in the pond.

After tea we began the long walk back through the wood. It was already dusk. We passed a family party and stood aghast while the father swung an 8 month old baby, stark naked, by one leg. Very strengthening, they said. I should think it must be. The ones that survive must be amazingly strong. When we got to the pond two women and Sasha, the most fanatical of the bunch, stripped off and leaped into it. Pausing only to worship life for a minute or two, standing on the brink, heads thrown back, arms stretched towards the sky. We waited in – well – awed respect just about describes it.

Finally we got to the other side of the wood. That was when I discovered that I'd left my handbag, with passport, money, keys and passes, in the house. Sasha offered to escort me. I waved off the group and started back through the wood. They had found the bag and were expecting me. The artist asked if he could paint my portrait, we exchanged a few cultural remarks about Bach, Scriabin and translating poetry. Then Sasha and I set off to walk through the wood again. It was, by now, pitch-black. There was no way of seeing the puddles of mud and yellow birch leaves. One walked straight through them. I took Sasha's arm as an alternative to falling down in them. In the middle of the wood he stopped. He could, if I liked, offer me some massage.

Ah, I thought. I am in this wood, in total darkness, in Moscow, with a lunatic. DON'T PANIC. I said coldly, in my primitive Russian – "I don't like massage. At all." He said he had only offered and we moved on. I was never more happy to see a trolley-bus. He kissed me as it arrived; not your farewell triple peck – straight on the mouth.' I might have used my unsayable word if I hadn't been so glad to get out of that damn wood.

My new life became everyday life, faster than I would have thought possible. Its main features were studying, finding food, translation, lots of theatre and getting it wrong. Perhaps getting it wrong made me feel more English; I decided to sign the book. I shopped at the embassy commissariat, got Alex to hold my tatty carrier, put on my gloves and walked into the main entrance. (If that sounds dangerously easy you should have seen the guard on the barred gates.)

This time I gave it the full Miss Marple. 'Do you still have a book?

If you do, I would like to sign it.' Perhaps it was my suggestion that standards were falling which needled her into letting me stay. I looked like a tramp. By now most of my clothes were filthy and I hadn't yet discovered a dry-cleaner. 'Signing the book' is of course, some sort of ancient right, relic of those 'grand tours' which young men used to take; there might have only been three Englishmen in Moscow at any one time and all of them knew the ambassador. It is not a right on which I was expected to insist. I sat in the marble entrance hall, hoped no one would notice the state of my shoes, and signed the huge red-leather bound book. 'Expected date of departure?' June '91. 'That ought to do it. No excuse at all. I expect an invitation within days'. And it came. Posted into their own office – the Cultural Section – and collected by student rota, as were all our letters. A stiff white card reading 'Her Britannic Majesty's Ambassador and Lady Braithwaite request the pleasure of the company of – me.' For lunch. On Saturday, the third of November at 1 p.m. 'I wore my dark-green tartan dress with the big silver brooch – very British. At first a Georgian conductor held forth. No other word for it. He spoke of terrible times, of Lavrenty Beria . No one interrupted him. Rodric and Jill Braithwaite dropped in sympathetic comments. They both speak fluent Russian. Afterwards I managed a conversation with the film-man sitting next to me. He'd been in London 3 weeks ago. I expressed surprise that it still existed and off we went ...

By about 4.30 there was an exodus (quietly stage-managed, no doubt). Where was I going? Would I like a lift? I suggested the nearest metro. Lady Braithwaite wouldn't hear of it. The Union Jack is removed from the Silver Spirit (only the ambassador may fly the flag) and I am driven by a uniformed chauffeur to the Pushkin Institute in a Rolls-Royce. I rather wish it had still been Sokolniki. I do love extremes.'

Vitia Borovskii, theatre-historian then teaching at SSEES, had given me something so generous; a letter of introduction to his cousin, the actor Sergei Iurskii. I'm trying to think how to describe him. 'Celebrated' gives you no idea of his warmth and – if you've never seen him – none at all of his gifts. I've watched him perform a Chekhov story involving a cook and a carp. He became the cook and I saw the carp. His wife, Natalia, my favourite Ranevskaia, kept me going by inviting me to the sort of meals I was beginning to forget; there was food in Moscow if you knew where to look for it. Though you'd have needed considerably more than a student stipend…

One afternoon, after such a lunch, she took me to the Tolstoy Museum. His Moscow home. 'Ulitsa L'va Tolstovo' - 'Street of Lev Tolstoy'. People always turn up in the genitive here. I can't explain what a powerful effect the place had on me. It's all there – just as he left it. They haven't even installed electricity. We tied on the obligatory cloth slippers over our shoes and shuffled off. Every room has its babushka, sitting there motionless. We were the only visitors. The light was beginning to go as we wandered from room to room. Up the wooden stairs to the dining room, laid for dinner with blue and white china – the music room with a grand, the family room where the eleven children put on plays and drank tea (Samovar on the sideboard, cups and saucers in place on the table). While Tolstoy read bits from the papers aloud to them ….. the rug made from the bear which nearly killed him when he was thirty. (We nearly missed 'War and Peace'. Makes the blood run cold.) ….. The boots he made for himself (obstinate old man, cursing away, insisting on doing it) and then his study. Small room, heavy buttoned leather sofa, dark green walls. A framed notice on the door-jamb said that this was where he wrote, among other things 'The Death of Ivan Ilyich'. Now this is very un-English of me and you're not to think I'm cracking up – but I looked at this desk and great sobs came up from the bottom somewhere and there was nothing I could do about it. Well – you know. University had slightly overlaid my original enthusiasm for Tolstoy – there was so much else that was new and exciting. Standing there in the half-light the whole thing came back to me. No, it wasn't alcohol. We didn't drink with lunch. After that the babushka got up and showed us everything.'

Translation was proceeding on an industrial scale. I had just finished the 41 poems and the first chapter of a novel when I was offered an opera libretto by a contemporary composer. Needed by the end of December. 'I may have to start turning stuff down' I wrote.

Can this really have been the first time it occurred to me? 'Or take a week off from the course to catch up. And we're off to Piatigorsk on Saturday – only for five days. I need the break. This ceaseless round of pleasure will do for me ....

Let me tell you about Piatigorsk. We flew there. Our guide from the Maurice Torez, a man called Vasili Vasilevich – or perhaps Mikhail Mikhailovich - escorted us to another hostel without food, some distance from the centre of town, and left. After a while even the cold water was cut off. Dafydd went to ask why. "This is the Soviet Union" he was told by the fierce woman who guarded our landing. They were short of water? We spent five days there, mostly rather hungry. But it always happens. Just as you are getting really angry they show you something so beautiful it takes your breath away.

We went by bus, a journey of 3 or 4 hours, up into the mountains. (It may have just felt like 3 or 4 hours). There I managed to hurl myself backwards into one of those single-chair ski lifts as it dangled past me, spotted the safety-chain just in time to fasten it before we wobbled upwards over what I can only describe as an abyss. It would not have been a good moment to discover that I had no head for heights. But the magnificence of those mountains, the dazzling snow in bright sunlight, blue shadows, tall dark trees, of course, but lower down little bare deciduous ones outlined in rime that looked like puffs of smoke. At the top we ate trout; they were brought in from the clearest stream I have ever seen and cooked for us. What can you do? I forgave Piatigorsk.' Just. 'We're on the plane! We got away! They're going to let us go back to Moscow! This whole plan was devised in order to make us realise how well off we are there, queues and all. Mind you, the plane hasn't started yet. They're still winding the elastic. Mineral Water airport takes do-it-yourself to new heights. No trolleys. No lifts. The waiting room (no option – that's where you wait) is up two huge flights of stairs. When I saw them I snapped. I shouted to anyone who cared to listen "If I die of a heart attack tell them I died furious." Then I humped my case up the stairs. What saved my life was a little bar up there that sold black coffee and would heat salami and cheese on bread. I had two of these and a piece of chocolate cake. I began to see that life had meaning.'

The winter came. In Moscow the little old ladies were kneeling on pieces of cardboard in the snow now, holding out icons. If they weren't selling strings of dried mushrooms in an underpass. The shops continued to empty. On 2nd January Lucy went into labour with her first child. I bought a bottle of champagne from the Vietnamese on the 13th floor of the Pushkin Institute (the Vietnamese could sell you anything) and took the metro to Dafydd's flat. It had a telephone. There I dozed off on a little wooden sofa in the kitchen until at 3 a.m. the phone rang. Lucy was safe, Oliver was a fine healthy baby. Dafydd joined me and we finished the bottle between us. In less than a fortnight I would see them both; we were due to fly home for a two-week break.

I had just finished the libretto when I noticed something fatal to my slowly growing comprehension of spoken Russian. Everything I heard now I translated into English. Translation had become a state of mind. Once I noticed this I constantly caught myself not listening to the second sentence because I was translating the first. It had to stop. I could see that: Reluctantly – because Detgiz, the publishers of the fairy-tales, were ready to publish anything else we cared to suggest – I told Marina and Victor that I would do no more translation after the break. They understood; I'd come to Moscow to fill my head with Russian. Now I was going home.

XIX

Everything was the same. The children were as loving as ever, the shops were full of food, London more wet than cold. It was I who had changed. I was like someone who had fallen in love, late and unexpectedly, and couldn't stop talking about it. I knew I should, but I didn't. And they were so kind. They let me go on about it endlessly, merely advising friends 'Don't mention the R-word.' (Russia was never the Soviet Union in the imagination; it just lay there under the snow, patiently waiting for the thaw).

I was beginning to feel like a proper grandmother again when the three weeks suddenly became two days and it was time to buy the lentils. I had been amazed by the precocity of Robert and Holly, held young Oliver in my arms and loved all of it; but I wanted to go back to Moscow and carry on with my adventure. What on earth could happen next?

I returned to the Pushkin with as many lentils as I could carry to a temperature of -32 degrees, unusual even in Moscow. I'd forgotten to put back the thermal insoles in my boots and my feet ached on the metal floor of the bus which took us there. When I had left the Pushkin the ladies in charge had offered to lock any of my valuables in the store room. Now I understood why. The rest of my stuff had been moved into a different double room; Irina had returned to Irkutsk and I was to share with a student who had rented a flat elsewhere. She was using the room as a dump, which she had visited some time ago to eat bread and oranges. I was sitting on the bed wondering where she got the oranges and if I had the energy to make the place habitable when Justine arrived, furious. 'I've told them,' she said. 'They're putting a bed in my room and you can share with me.' 'Wonderful,' I told her. 'It'll be like the old days.' It didn't seem possible that the old days were only four months ago.

Back at the Maurice Torez we had been allotted an extremely interesting lecturer. His subject was 'Utopianism in the 20th century'.

Everything from Hitler's national socialism to Mao Tse-tung so far. Am I really hearing this? I asked myself. Then phoned all my friends and started to fill up my diary. I had so much more time since I abandoned translation; I missed it, but its absence did stop me thinking in English, and I saw a lot more of Moscow. The church where Pushkin was married, for instance. Or rather, the shell of it – it had been used as a research laboratory for years. 'I gave three roubles to the restoration fund and lit a candle. Nina, herself a militant atheist, bought one each. So the two of us lit these candles and I got told off by the resident babushka for failing to remove my gloves. Then to the Gorkii Museum, a house built for Riabushinskii at the beginning of the century. A marvellous example of art nouveau. I would tell you all about it but guide books do it so much better – and more accurately. I will just mention the marble wave that accompanied the stairs up to the first floor and the thought that this was hardly the place in which to write socialist realism. Could he have refused to live in it? They say not. Poor man.

After a couple of weeks we moved to a new hostel, or obshchezhitie, affectionately known to the students as 'the Ob,', as in 'See you back at the Ob.' It was new. Literally new. We were its first occupants. It was cockroach-free and only five minutes' walk from the Maurice Torez, even less to the metro – Park Kul'tury. (The nearby park bears the splendid title 'Park of culture and rest in the name of M. Gorkii; in other words Gorkii Park). The Ob did have one or two disadvantages – it wasn't quite finished. But it had all the essentials. I particularly remember the bed. It was the sort I had slept on in my boarding-school, a frame of crossed wires supporting the traditional blue and white stripey flock mattress. It sagged. Fortunately most of the students had rented themselves accommodation by now; for them this was a novelty. I dismantled two spare beds and put the head-boards under the mattress. The effect was kind but firm; a slipped disc would have been no problem.

'Another minute disadvantage is that the only phones – two of them – are on the outside of the building. So that a phone call involves putting on a woolly scarf, fur coat, fur hat, fur boots, fur gloves, then tramping three yards through the snow and trying to get the money in without dropping it, dialling, and getting back into the gloves before your hands freeze. I tell you – they like problems. Where would be the fun if some earnest thinker found them a solution? Come to think of it, one did. I leave you to draw the Lady Bracknell conclusion.

I asked our commandant (honestly, that's what they call her. Commandant. But they'll let me out in June. I promise) if someone was going to clean my room and if not could I have some means of cleaning it myself? I was given the neatly bound bunch of twigs, short enough to ensure that every housewife is permanently stooped in a grovelling position, and a piece of an old curtain. As that Georgian said at Nina's the other day "Scratch a Russian and you'll find a peasant." They're full of original sayings like that. Ah, don't knock them. They've had such a terrible time. They come from a broken Union. Nevertheless, the next Russian who says to me – proudly – "You don't know what problems are in the West" – will get it.'

We don't, of course. Not problems of the all-embracing helpless hopeless nature that the friends of my age in Russia have lived through. Problems that could make children betray their parents and parents save their children by disowning them. Read Vasili Grossman's 'Life and Fate'. Read Vitalii Shentalinskii's 'Slaves of Freedom', the first of three books that preserve the letters, the   dossiers, the memory of the repressed writers. Read Orlando Figes' 'The Whisperers' to see how ordinary people survived. And if you find my jokes inappropriate in the circumstances you should hear the Russians.

Vitali, scientist turned poet, and his wife Tania, folklorist and musicologist, were to become friends for life. Vitali, dedicated to the cause of the repressed writers, had arranged an evening in their honour at the 'Dom Literatorov', and I was invited. 'Many of these writers had died in the gulag, but some of the survivors read their own stuff. The first poet, an old man, hands shaking, went on too long. The chairman/compère asked him to remember "our other friends sitting on the platform". He stopped, and left. Another bearded poet stamped off. I thought he'd come out in sympathy but Tania whispered that he thought he should have spoken first. One elderly man sang his poems to his own guitar accompaniment. I was struck by the really beautiful way he produced his pianissimo; it seems that he had learned his technique from a very famous singer in the camps. Afterwards we walked back to their flat in the snow – underfoot and falling fairly fast ….. Drank vodka and tea and talked.' There was plenty to talk about; I had seen the hall in the 'Dom Literatovov' where the committee met to expel Pasternak from the writers' union. 'Then they took me by tram to the metro and I arrived back at the new hostel – so near, no bus journey – at one o'clock in the morning to find the door locked. I rattled and banged till the 'militsioner' on duty opened up ….. God, but what a day. I'd already visited the church on the corner, the one whose bells I hear. The place was packed. Not only with babushki – young people too. A blaze of candles, gilt everywhere, good sophisticated singing (a small choir with conductor) – no nonsense about the congregation joining in. I gave my rouble for the restoration fund and walked over the bridge to Gorkii Park to see the ice-sculptures.'

It must have been at about this point that Gorbachov decided to ask the people in a referendum: what kind of a Soviet Union do you want? Because I met an old lady sitting on a bench in the metro. 'Supposing she was 70. Born in '21. Brought up during NEP. Out-lived Stalin, the lot. Imagine the level of faith and enthusiasm of her parents. "They governed us properly before all that perestroika" she said. "Shops – full of everything you could want." (The camps were pretty full too, I thought, but said nothing). "Referendum – pah!" she spat through her gold teeth. I gave her my opinion that the majority would vote to preserve some sort of Soviet Union (however changed, renewed, restored – to quote various papers) and we parted friends. If my grandchildren were her grandchildren I'd be worried. That I did tell her. Don't forget, I'll be in Riga on the 17th – referendum day. Just in case Moscow erupts.' This was the view held by several of the students; they were getting us out of Moscow in case we decided to join in. I can think of one or two who might have done.

'We'd been sent to stay, not in Riga, but 40 minutes away by local train at a health resort on the coast – Iurmola. Excellent pensionat. Three minutes from sea. Through pine trees to a pale sandy shore with sea still frozen at the edges. Water mirror-calm. Fun to stand on frozen sea. Climb over the chunks of ice, admire the thin wandering line of it decorating the very edge of the water, gaze into nothingness, breathe the pure air. Well. You know me. Two hours of that is enough. After 2 hours I longed for Moscow.' Onegin lasted a little longer on his newly-inherited country estate.

The lonely fields' pale evening gleam,
The ancient oak groves, cool and dim,
The murmur of the gentle stream,
For two days all seemed new to him.
But on the third the sight of all
Those hills and dales began to pall.

I know how he felt.

'We went to a concert of organ music in the Cathedral – fine building, excellent organ, 'naff' music. First half was Mendelssohn. At least bearable. Second half was like that stuff they play on steam-organs in fairgrounds. There was even a cymbal.' I must intervene to tell you that this was the grossest slander and indicates the depth of my disappointment. I was craving for Bach. Please bear this in mind when you read 'after which we were taken out to a bad expensive meal with a cringe-makingly bad cabaret. When the dancers went topless I thought Francesca, our most ardent feminist and women's-libber, would stage a one-woman demo. It was quite the funniest bit of the evening.' Thinking of Riga now I remember the sea, frozen at the edges; can this really have been what I saw? I remember an elegant bridge suspended on multiple swooping arcs which looked like a pencil drawing; most of all I remember the group of little children who raced happily about our hotel corridors, laughing and shouting; they were from Chernobyl.'

The winter left. Mounds of dirty snow thawed into even dirtier sludge and finally dribbled away. Easter Sunday was on 7th April in '91. Russian Orthodox Easter. Friends invited me to accompany them to the midnight mass at Novodevichii Monastery. We met at eleven. 'Huge crowds. Militia moving metal barriers about to direct them. A certain amount of 'khamstvo' - oh, general boorishness – on the part of the young soldiers and an overwhelming mass of believers. Choral singing, holding thin red candles stuck through paper to catch the drips, icons carried in procession, a way through the crowd cleared for them by militia, representatives of the atheist state. At midnight the singing rises to a shout of "Christ is risen" from the priest and the answering cry "In truth He is risen". Then the cathedral bells ring in the resurrection. Impressive.

Home on the metro – just in time – the bit I need closes at one. Back at the Ob the young men sitting at the desk in the entrance hall check my pass and give me back the key to my room. Young policemen – militia, in uniform. "Christ is risen", one of them said. For a split second I thought I must have misheard him. Then "In truth he is risen" I agreed. What a fine pair of atheists. We should both be struck off …

I have just spent five hours in the Stomatological Polyclinic No. 8. To you – the dentist. I don't know if you remember the bit in those briefing documents that went "If, God forbid, you should need dentistry …"? Well this was where they, and God, were forbidding you to go for it. But I had bitten on a reckless nut and broken a crown. Nina (head-mistress Nina) said she had a friend who was a dentist, an expert in prosthetics. I imagined a private dentist. She doesn't speak English, which is probably why I didn't realise till we got there and she introduced me to him that he's the head of dentistry in a vast state-run polyclinic. However, I'd brought my needles and laid down a bottle of cognac for tactful presentation later so I thought I'd give it a go.

Lev Nikolaevich put on a white coat, a white hat, washed his hands for a while, looked at my mouth. "Why are you not using a lower-jaw prosthesis?" – he asked. "You are overloading those teeth." He was, of course, absolutely right. I promised to try and stick in all those wretched extra back teeth. He escorted me to another surgery. I could see trays of syringes. This was IT. If I didn't want AIDS I'd got to get this bit right. I'd got my own needles in my shoulder-holster with passport and money, for quick access. A woman came at me, syringe poised. The hell with courtesy. 'Are those new disposable needles? If not, I have my own.' They were. I could see. Little paper strips of them, just like mine. After two injections I was blissfully numb, adrenalin-packed.

To another surgery. The treatment one. Three chairs, homely atmosphere – bits of chocolate cake and somebody's cold tea on the shelf, a plateful of bread, a bunch of wilting herbs. No water-cooled drills, apparently, but as each woman (they were all women apart from Lev Niolaevich) was treating two or three patients, by the time it was your turn again the mouth was totally dead. They couldn't find what they were looking for. God knows they tried. The dentist said the radiographer was useless. At the fourth x-ray I protested. Was it absolutely necessary? They explained to me that these Roentgen rays weren't proper Roentgen rays, just some kind of weak, harmless variety; I'd been up the two flights of stairs to the x-ray department three times already, but I began to suspect that if they didn't get a move-on the injections would wear off. I went up a fourth time. It came out beautifully. One for the album. Everybody was pleased.

Downstairs to pay for the treatment. Eighteen roubles and some kopeks. Upstairs to a different cashier to pay in advance for the crown. Forty-five roubles and some kopeks. We're talking real money here. That's very nearly a pound.

At a quarter to eight – five hours after I arrived – I staggered out. Tomorrow – if I can find my way back to room 13 and the large woman in the blue paper hat – I can have my crown. She said. She's making it for me'. That was 23 years ago and I have had no trouble whatsoever with that crown. It's still going strong. Clearly an excellent piece of work. My apologies to the lovely lady in the blue paper hat.

XX

In April a series of excursions began, the first of them to Bukhara. Nineteen students in shorts and tee-shirts in joyous expectation of blazing heat, me in my linen coat and skirt and my summer hat – a sort of wicker solar topee. It came on to snow as we left in a bus for the airport. It snowed so heavily that all flights were cancelled. 'We picked our way through ankle-deep sludge to the departure lounge like a bunch of extras who'd strayed onto the wrong set. My solar topee looked particularly fine with a layer of snow.' I took over an armchair – there were only a few – but most of the students slept on the stone floor. They were at least luckier than the two goats in a box, left bleating all night. In the morning that thing a giant hair-dryer on a truck blew the snow off our plane and we flew to Bukhara.

'I had heard that there wasn't an airport in Bukhara. I'm still not sure. It was like landing in somebody's rather large garden. Very pleasant. The hotel was good too...

Next morning, the conducted tour of Bukhara. Lots of yellowish sandstone. Oxford and Cambridge blue mosaics. Domes. Minarets. Tombs. Flat dusty bits and tall shaky bits.' What could those have been? The effect of the heat? 'Local young men leering at slim young students in shorts, local old men looking disgusted. A stone step laid out with copper and brass pots and jugs. I bought a jug for 80 roubles. He asked 100. I offered 75. He refused. I started to walk away. He asked what I would pay. I said 80 was my absolute last offer. He agreed. Probably worth all of 20. But it's hard to take roubles seriously. An ancient copper jug for about £1.70. Instead of £2.10. I was only haggling for the fun of it and because it's expected. When I've read the guide book I'll tell you what I saw. Whatever it was, I'm sure I'd like it better by moonlight.' The jug is beautiful. I filled it with bird-sand and I use it as a book-end on my writing table. 'After dinner – cool, dark, bliss – a few of us ate coffee ice cream and drank champagne in the garden of the hotel. The nights are definitely the best bit.'

On the following day, more sight-seeing; we went by bus to Lake Tudakul. 'Arrived to find Mos-film using the plage. Our bus driver found a stretch of beach; rough grass, sand, stones, a wide border of dry reeds. Cold blue water. Really cold when you plunge in from that heat. It was gorgeous till I got out and saw the catch. No shade. Everyone prepared to sunbathe; I draped a towel over some tough dried branches of something growing through the reeds. A young man – one or two local residents had come there to swim – sent his girlfriend over to say: "Greetings! There are snakes in those reeds." I leapt up, took a bottle of mineral water and headed for the bus. The driver had laid a mat in its shade and was fast asleep. I didn't have a bottle opener. I thought I'd wait till thirst overcame my natural politeness. Then wake him up. Fortunately his mate, who'd been swimming, came back to the bus and saved me from social disgrace.

Friday – our last day. Here's the plan. We are woken at 4.30 a.m., leave at 5, spend 10 hours in the bus to Tashkent, stopping at one or two notable places along the way. We are then taken by the bus on an excursion round Tashkent. Back to the airport by 7 p.m. Flight leaves at 9 p.m.

Now. Here's what actually happened. They woke us at 4.30. We sat in the bus till 6 (the mineral water hadn't arrived), then set off at a bone-shaking pace. (Did I tell you our driver got stopped for speeding on the way to the airport in Moscow? With a bus like that this was a real achievement.)' I had evidently not yet understood that the police, too, must make a living. 'Samarkand we only saw from a distance. A visit was part of the plan, but the driver took the Samarkand by-pass and chose to stop, 20 minutes later, in a small, grim village. Still, I wouldn't have missed it for the world. There are not many people who can say that they've been to the worst public lavatory in Central Asia. It was a small stone building, open on one side, buzzing with flies, standing in a desolate yard behind the village store, a good thirty yards from the kebab-stall. I'm used to a hole in the ground but this had stopped being a hole. I stood there and thought – "For this I missed Samarkand." I expect the driver had a cousin there. There has to be a reason. (Wrong, wrong, wrong. Of course there doesn't have to be a reason. This is fatalist territory.)

We arrived on time, at 3 p.m., in Tashkent. That was where the plan really went wrong. The bus-driver wasn't staying. He off-loaded us onto the pavement in front of the airport and left. I hope he and his cousin eat lots of the kebabs from that stall.

Justine and Dafydd and I set out to see something of Tashkent on foot, but the heat defeated us. As a consequence, the only thing I remember about Tashkent is the customs officer at the airport; he made me unpack every bit of my luggage because the fruit-knife I'd brought with me had been detected at the bottom of it. A terrorist granny with a fruit-knife? I know, I know. He was only doing his job. And I'm back in lovely cold, grey, rainy Moscow now.

Suddenly everything went green and I was filled with the urge to explore. I started to wander round the Boulevarde Circle, bit by bit, with time to take little side roads. Off Pushkin Square I found Chekhov Street, where he lived in three different houses. No. 29 was a small, square dolls' house in the classical Moscow manner, yellow painted plaster with white stonework round doors and windows. A little derelict, chipped and fading with a bronze plaque. No. 11 was on the corner of an alley which led to a gloomy little park, full of cast-iron lamp standards, urns and statues. There was a summer house for reading in. It said so, over the door. And another, more enclosed, for writing and playing chess. Green, fresh, raining. My kind of place. It's called Monastery Garden. At the studio-theatre in the middle of it they were playing 'Dr Zhivago'. I bought a ticket and, with time to kill, went for a stroll. Found the monastery where Peter the Great, as a boy, having escaped from the Kremlin, hid during that ferocious palace coup. Found – even more important – a tiny shop where I bought an unheard of luxury, hitherto unobtainable and not provided by the hostel – a dustpan. I've got the bundle of twigs; now I've got the dustpan to go with it. What will they think of next?

I left it in the garderobe with my umbrella and watched this enormous novel come to life on a small central rostrum, the action spilling over onto the stairs dividing the 4 blocks of seats surrounding it. And the pianist played, among other things, my Prokofiev gavotte.

The one with all the 9ths that he dedicated to Tatisha's father and I'm always playing. I noticed that he stopped before the difficult bit at the end and went off into a flourish of chords instead. Oh my God. I'll admit to being tired. But what a year. I hope something wonderful and unexpected happens to you all when you're 64 and thinking you've done it all and what more could change?'

I wrote twenty-seven letters to my children during those ten months, most of them ten to twelve pages long, not one of them dated. Fortunately I numbered them all. Once or twice, however, I dated an event. May 18th '91 for instance. That was the day I saw Lenin and heard Richter. Time was running out; we were due to leave Moscow at the end of June and I decided to join the long queue outside the mausoleum. 'Well you have to'. I wrote. We filed down into the vault in the deepest silence. Self-imposed, though there were soldiers ready to impose it. Four of them stood on guard, immobile, one at each corner, the man himself beautifully lit, looking the picture of health.

I had tea with Nina – dear headmistress Nina, long since dead. I told her that I had seen Lenin, unprepared for the powerful emotion this evoked. 'What did you think?' she asked me with tears in her eyes. I didn't want to lie to her; faith deserves respect. 'It was very impressive' I told her. At least that was true.

That evening I heard Richter. I had phoned everyone I knew to get a ticket – they'd all been sold before I heard of the concert – but Tania Shentalinskii got us two via the Union of Composers. Richter was already a sick man and hadn't played for several months. 'He performed two Bach concertos while young students of the Conservatoire stood round him, a chamber orchestra in the old manner. It was beautiful, simple, transparent playing. You only heard the Bach.'

Now it was nearly June, our last month in Moscow. We had completed the course at the Maurice Torez - well Dafydd and I had – but there was one more excursion planned for us. To Ust Kamenogorsk; try 'oost', then gabble through the first three syllables of the second word and land with a thump on 'gorsk'. You have to admire the organisers of our ten months; seventy-five years of certainty disintegrating at an ever-increasing pace and there they are sticking to the deal and sending us on excursions. I did love that Institute. I went and spoke to a roomful of teachers and students there about three years ago. They gave me such a welcome. Heart-stopping.

Ust Kamenogorsk is 2,274 miles from Moscow and only 993 miles from Mongolia; it had been a closed city. We were welcomed by young men with flowers at the airport as the very first foreigners to set foot in it. 'Welcomed' doesn't quite describe it; I stayed with a mother and her young daughter who looked after me and fed me as though I were one of their own. Our guide and constant companion was an English teacher, Tamara, who had never spoken to an actual English person. Her English was fluent and correct, her conversation peppered with slightly dated idioms. Her favourite was 'and what-not'; she left an awful lot of sentences dangling with that one. Her determination to acquire my accent was unflagging. If she could have had it out of me by surgery she would have been tempted. What a lovely woman. On our last evening she and 7 or 8 friends hired the small local sauna and invited me to join them. 'I lay there on this wooden shelf and asked Tamara "Is it all right? My thighs have gone a funny colour. Like salami – blotchy red and white." She said "Yes, it's the heat." Ah well. After alternately baking myself senseless and plunging into a very cold pool for a while, she said that it was time to rest. I envisaged a quiet dark room where I would lie and recover. Not a bit of it. They had prepared a banquet. We were still wrapped in our towels and wearing woolly hats (essential protection at that temperature), in addition to which my face was covered in smetana – soured cream – which Tamara had assured me would heal my burned face in no time. We sat round the table together and laid in to herring fillets, smoked fish, marinated mushrooms, cake – there must have been cake – their traditional dish which I think was called something like 'Besh Parmak (pasta and lamb, absolutely delicious, hot fragrant stuff); I might have remembered the name properly but for the cognac, wine and vodka with which we drank numerous toasts to friendship; among nations, of course, but more importantly among us. Ladies, it was magnificent. I thank you from the bottom of my heart. I was still recording English for Tamara onto a cassette-recorder next morning when half the students were already on the airport bus.

I wish I could have gone back.

My last letter from the Soviet Union was headed:

'The Trans-Siberian Express,

Thursday, June 13th, 1991'

I hadn't often had the chance to head letters with such exotica and I was making the most of it. This was an expedition that Dafydd and I had planned for ourselves. To be fair, Dafydd did most of the planning – he was so good at it. Later he and his partner Renaud would plan me such expeditions; to Belgium, Paris, New York, even Pretoria; this last to meet their little adopted son, Marc. But Irkutsk was the first one.

'All my Russian friends said "Don't do it. You're mad." Except Sergei Iurskii. He knew that I wanted to understand this country. Not just as a tourist.' I don't think you can ever get right under the skin of another culture; but the attempt is the thing. I have met such people and had such fun and tried so many things that would once have seemed impossible.

Irina had invited us to come and stay with her and Sasha and meet their two boys. We could, of course, have flown there in 5 hours, but the lure of the Trans-Siberian Railway was irresistible. I wanted to feel the immensity of what was still, to me, Russia; travel by plane makes nothing of distance. The rouble was in a bad way and that memorable journey, four nights on the train, cost the equivalent of eight pounds. We took food and water with us, and the samovar at the end of the corridor was always boiling. There didn't seem to be any other foreigners on the train and our presence in this four-berth coupé appeared to deter Russians; no one else joined us. A young man who got on at Omsk climbed up in silence to a top bunk but I offered him vodka and he left. I was only trying to be friendly; perhaps he thought I had put something in it. Drugging drinks as a preliminary to robbery was not unknown on these long-distance trains.

We progressed at a determined saunter past stone houses, brick houses, wooden houses, into a land which seemed to have no houses at all. Only sunny birch-groves. Day after day after day of them. Very occasionally Dafydd would shout 'Look! There's someone! On a bike.

There. No, he's gone.' I began to feel that there could be whole villages surrounded by those birch-groves that had never heard about the revolution.

Irkutsk was an unexpected oasis. The Decembrists, educated young idealists whose earlier attempt at one landed them in the Siberian salt-mines, were allowed to settle in Irkutsk on their release. Their attempt to create a Petersburg in exile has left its mark. Theatres, art galleries, a flourishing university, wooden houses, smaller but quite as elegant as their stone mansions in the capital, now museums in their name. Irina and Sasha welcomed us so warmly and entertained us with such Siberian hospitality; it seems ungracious to record that in a temperature of plus 40 degrees I got heat stroke and missed the last party. I still feel a twinge of regret.

We flew back to Moscow on the following day, back to the near empty supermarkets with their empty shelves, empty cabinets; some very pink sausage, perhaps, or large jars of apple juice. Occasionally bread. A queue of women would form at the bread bin and wait for loaves to be hurled out into it from the opening in the wall behind, curtained with plastic strips 'I'm not saying anything,' one elderly teacher had told us. 'Just remember. The women were queuing for bread before the last revolution.' But the young lecturer was also right. 'Cheer up. You can go home' he had said. And on the 29th June, 1991, just two months before the first coup, we did.

I know that between leaving Irkutsk and going back to London Dafydd and I visited Leningrad. I know we did. But I was mostly asleep or at best semi-conscious. I could not do justice to this creation of Peter, now once again Petersburg. However much Pushkin loved it I still prefer Moscow. Moscow gave me my golden time (Sonnet 3) and as golden times should, it changed everything.

XXI

I had come back from the Soviet Union resistant to the idea of finals. Life in London seemed too easy. Penny-plain. I missed my tuppence-coloured Moscow, I missed Marina's kitchen. And where was the fun in finding a cabbage in a supermarket full of cabbages? Then I went to the library at SSEES. There is something about books, specially old ones, though even new ones send out a signal. I sat there for a bit, breathing them in, remembering this other kind of excitement; then I went home to my Dostoevsky summer. I had finally chosen Dostoevsky and Bulgakov as my two 'special authors' for finals without considering the length of your average Dostoevsky novel or my decision to read the whole course in Russian. Still, at fifty pages a day they would only take about a fortnight each. I decided to stay in bed every morning until I'd read the fifty pages. It seemed a sensible plan.

The books I had bought in Moscow all arrived over the summer. In the Moscow of 1991 I had been, for the first and last time in my life, a wealthy woman. There were at least 200 of them; ten 'Complete Collected Works' of all my favourite 19th century authors, an equal quantity of novels, poems, short stories, books on the language - I specially like the one titled 'Stress in Russian' – dictionaries, including Marina's gift, the four volumes of Dal', reprinted in 1989. Posted to Nikolaev on the Black Sea, Dal', then an eighteen-year-old naval warrant officer, started to list all the words not previously known to him. A week before his death in 1872, he asked his daughter to include four new words which he had just heard from a servant in what was already the second edition of his great dictionary. I didn't realise when Marina gave it to me how valuable it would be to me, so I thought I'd celebrate it here. Back to the books.

The twenty volumes of Saltykov-Shchedrin which Dafydd found for me and lugged back to the hostel must have filled two or three parcels. Most of them had been packed for me in the parcel office, just round the corner from Tsentral'nii Telegraf. Every volume was scrutinised; pre-packed parcels were not accepted. Seventy-five of the books were brought to London by a visiting group of schoolgirls, whose headmistress, my friend Nina Nikolaevna, arranged for them to take three each to the school in London where they were to be based and where – a most fortunate coincidence – Sarah's husband worked. I started on the Dostoevsky as soon as the ten volumes arrived, reading through mornings which sometimes lasted until 3 o'clock in the afternoon, breaking off occasionally to make more coffee and taking an apple, a sandwich, anything you could hold in the hand that wasn't holding a book, back to bed. I lived in his mad world of jaw-dropping complexity until, for a few glorious months, I could hold it all in my head and think from one work to another. It didn't last of course.

I'll leave you to imagine the excessive zeal, driven by panic, with which I revised for finals. There were to be eight three hour papers spread over two weeks in which I was to   remember everything I had learned in the last four years. I couldn't even remember where I'd put my glasses. I stayed in Bob's London pad during those two weeks – it was a five minute walk from SSEES – with the mountain of books I considered necessary. I remember swimming every day in the Students' Union pool (you'll be glad to hear I was a union member) which was like swimming in an aggressive stew. I remember taking bottles of water and glucose tablets in to the examination halls; it may have been against the rules but I placed them in full view on my table and no one challenged me. Most of all I remember the exhilarating high as the dam burst and all the stuff I had balanced in my head came pouring out onto the paper. Unnatural woman. I am a bit ashamed of enjoying it. But it's true, so I feel obliged to tell you. Matthew took me and my books back to Catford. Incoherent, white-faced and staring, he said.

I got the first. I waited for the confidence which this was to inspire. It didn't come. That was when I finally thought the hell with confidence. I'll do it anyway. So that when Arnold – Professor McMillin - who had given us the memorable Dostoevsky course took me out to lunch and suggested a PhD, I agreed. I hadn't the slightest idea what it would involve but I was flattered by the suggestion and I was enjoying the lunch.

I applied for funding and was turned down. I was sixty-seven by then and I could see that there were young people with careers to make. They had already paid for me to do a degree while I was drawing my pension; what more did I want? A PhD. I spent a year trying every feasible source, talked to my MP, went to see the Mayor of Lewisham, Sinna Mani. He took me seriously. 'They need someone to do interviews for Black History Month. Any good?' He sent me to the appropriate department and they took me on. I was so grateful – I still am. I borrowed a little hand-held recorder, made a list of what I thought might be suitable questions and went to meet the first family. Six generations of Vietnamese women, their ages ranging from 102 to 3. Only the nineteen-year-old spoke English and she had forgotten to come. They were so kind. They gave me tea. We sat and smiled a lot. A passing boy on a bicycle who spoke both languages was called in to help arrange another appointment and I went home with different questions, the answers to which would fill a different book.

In the following year I began work on a part-time PhD. I had imagined it to be a continuation of the degree course only more so. Wrong. Not lessons and lectures and discussions and laughter and the constant companionship of friendly, interesting people; just you and your subject. And your own company. It's as well that Arnold agreed to be my supervisor or I might have given up. I began by choosing the wrong subject. I had only read one book by Saltykov-Shchedrin – the one that all students read, 'The Golovlievs'. It was the blackest, funniest book. I started on the rest of the twenty volumes expecting more of the same and began to reconsider the first one. With a sinking feeling. Had I completely misinterpreted it? Was S.S. not the wicked old cynic I had taken him for? Apparently not. I read on, nevertheless, cheering myself up by finishing my translation of Griboedov's 'Woe from Wit', most of which I had written during my search for funding. It took me the whole year to see the obvious. If I was going to spend all that time alone with somebody I'd rather spend it with Griboedov; I applied for and received permission to change my subject.

It must have been 1994 before I returned to Moscow. I was

frightened to risk it; going back held the possibility of disillusion. It was something I had done that was over and could not be repeated. Wrong again. I had barely started. Moscow was to become somewhere else I lived. In 1994 my 'Woe from Wit' translation won me the prize offered in this country by the Griboedov Trust – a cash prize and a ticket to Russia with an invitation to take part in his bicentenary celebrations in January '95. And to speak at the conference. All this would take place in what had been his uncle's estate in Viazma, Smolensk, where Griboedov had spent his summer holidays as a boy; the great house had become a museum with a conference hall. Now I had to go back.

Reading a paper was pushing 'do it anyway' to the limits. I wrote it in my customary black ink and pencilled in all the stress-marks. 'Stress in Russian' is actually no joke. It is unstable, wanders about in an arbitrary manner and getting it wrong renders you incomprehensible. I would probably be incomprehensible anyway but at least the stresses would be in the right place. I tried it out here on a couple of Russians who looked doubtful and flew to Moscow in early January.

I love the cold. You can think in it. I sat in Dafydd's Moscow flat overlooking the frozen river, watched the mercury falling in the thermometer on the wall outside the kitchen window and exulted in that sense of renewal more often associated with spring. I lay in bed in the early morning and listened to my favourite sound – the ice and compacted snow being scraped from the pavements. Then I joined the bus-load of academics and travelled through the countryside in winter – the memory is making me homesick as I write – to the estate once owned by Griboedov's uncle. His serf theatre is gone but the small private church, like the house, has been lovingly restored by the architect Viktor Kulakov. I have held a lighted candle and been undeservedly blessed in that church. It was a clear case of Toad in the smoking-room; 'I'd say anything in there.'

I think we spent five days in Khmelita. Perhaps a week. I had been invited to stay with Viktor's female colleagues in one of the wings, opposite rather than attached to the house, which was so much more friendly than a lonely hotel room in Viazma. The snow was deep that year but a path had been carved out to the great house, so I walked each morning to breakfast in a two-foot deep trench.

Russian conferences are, of course, different to ours. Why would they not be? Nevertheless, their informality came as a pleasant surprise. Questions were sometimes asked – and answered – before the speaker had finished speaking and invited them. I was warned that if people got bored they had been known to talk amongst themselves. I was at least spared this fate; I think it took all their concentration to try and understand what I was saying and they very kindly made the effort. There was even a concert at which I read my translation of the hero's last monologue in 'Woe from Wit'. I remembered declaiming Derzhavin at the Maurice Torez and did my damnedest. It went down well; I think they understood me better in English. After the concert there was, of course, the final party. It took place at the house Viktor had built himself near his life's work. Good food, good company, numerous toasts. I seem to remember Viktor singing. At one point we accompanied him to the cow-shed. 'Got to milk the cows', he told us. 'My cowman died. Only young. We couldn't get the medicine'. On the way out he took a silver tea-glass holder from a shelf and gave it to me. 'For your translation' he said. 'It was my grandmother's'.

A feeling of despairing affection has just impelled me to put down my pen and reach for the tea-glass holder on the tray in front of me. I use it every morning when I write.

A pattern was established. I would spend several weeks in Moscow every year, always from mid-January to the end of February. First at Dafydd's Moscow flat overlooking the river, then, when he went home to a job in the cabinet office, with Marina. My circle of friends grew by the year.

Meanwhile, I worked at my thesis, the children at their weddings and marriages. Weddings are so beautiful. And marriages are so difficult. It's the reckless optimism. The swearing never to change when everything else does. 'Love is not love that alters when it alteration finds.' Well yes, but...supposing it wasn't alteration you'd found but what had always been reality? Of course, when marriages succeed they're beautiful too. Howard and Eve, for instance. Their marriage survived a year of silence between them when Howard left the communist party a year before Eve did. It was the year between Hungary and Czechoslovakia and Eve told him he was a class traitor. There must have been so many miracles of forbearance of which I can know nothing.

Emma decided to end her first marriage; there were good reasons - the best. Her second marriage was a different affair entirely. How different came as something of a shock. There was the rapturous first meeting, the wedding (beautiful) and a year or two later the revelation, which Emma kept from everyone but Sarah for another year.

Then I was invited to lunch. Emma and Sarah met me at the station and I got into the back of the car with Holly (Sarah's) and Ellie (Emma's). No one spoke. I thought: are they angry with me about something? Have they just had the most enormous row? Then Emma told me. Her husband, her talk dark handsome husband, could no longer live as a man. He was, knew that he was and had always known that he was, a woman. They were going to stay together.

I might not have written about this had Emma not already published her own account of it in her book 'If you really loved me' as in 'If you really loved me you wouldn't do this' versus 'If you really loved me you'd support me through it'. She did. Every painful inch of the way. Then the woman left. At the age of four that little child had asked 'why aren't I like the other girls?' She was female then and she is now. I accepted her as a woman. I thought Emma brave to heroic but what I cared about was her happiness; if she was determined to make this work I would believe that it could. After I had pointed out to her now-partner that gender was key information and should have been imparted before any proposal of marriage. One angry conversation seemed better than something unsaid festering poisonously. I thought we had developed a friendship. I had read her early poems; now I understood the despair in them. I felt some small part of Emma's shock and sense of betrayal when she left.

Let me tell you something cheerful. It happened in the early days of the above marriage. Sarah, after an earlier divorce, had been living with her present partner for seven or eight years. She too invited me to lunch and said that I could dress up a bit if I liked. They were going to. They'd found this really good restaurant...I sat in the back of the car with Holly and thought my God it must be good. She's wearing a tiara. A very delicate, unobtrusive, in-among-the-hair tiara. But a tiara. I wished I hadn't worn my awful coat from the men's department in Moscow. I thought it was going to rain. We pulled into a car-park. Sarah turned to me and said 'Mum, we've got something to tell you. We're going to be married.' I still didn't get it. 'You couldn't have told me anything that would make me happier. When?' 'Now', she said and we fell about laughing. I felt such an idiot. I left the coat in the car and we went into the registry office. Emma her husband and her daughter Ellie joined us there. We had the wedding. Then we had the lunch in the really good restaurant.

Emma's second wedding had taken two years to organise; there was the special permission to be obtained for the ceremony in a Catholic church - they were both Catholics. I was interviewed by a nun. All this apart from the dress, the bridesmaids, the magnificent wedding breakfast. Sarah's wedding surely makes it unnecessary to tell you that my twins are not identical. They are utterly different and inseparably close.

Then there was Matthew's wedding. Fiona another lovely bride and Matthew, eccentric to the last in a royal blue zoot suit with a jacket that came down to his knees - a tribute to the forties swing he loved, the music to which he danced with such joyous lust. I was so happy on that day. I remembered driving to the registry office and hitting a gate post on the way in. Part of the bumper fell off but I left it in the road. Happy in charge of a vehicle - like drunk but without the alcohol.

And Lucy. She looked so beautiful in her cream silk dress with pale yellow roses in her hair. Neil 'gave her away' in a wheelchair pushed by Matthew. She had two children by then; Oliver, born in 1991 while I was in Moscow, and Ali in the following year. The first father didn't wait for the birth and the second left soon after it. Lucy was a single mother. There is, of course, no such thing as a single mother. Mostly just a feckless man somewhere else and a woman doing everything. The first father was merely irresponsible; the second was a professional con-man. When the house in which she had rented a room for herself and her son was repossessed Kent County Council found her a place in a bed-and- breakfast. The con-man was running it. A clerical error presumably. No one had checked his lengthy criminal record which included bank robbery and G.B.H. He was good at his job - I lent him fifty pounds.

When in 1997 a third man appeared there was talk of marriage. I was invited to meet him. We drank tea together and he told me such a ludicrous, unconvincing lie. How I wish I had known anything about Autism when Lucy was growing up; late diagnosis - at forty-eight in her case - can be too late; she was beginning to look like a really bad chooser.

Nevertheless. I helped her plan the wedding. We found the beautiful dress in one of those second - hand shops that sells such special things and we prepared the food together. Lucy made a mountain of profiteroles. She was not looking happy. Paler by the day. Not like a person about to do the one thing she really wanted to do. Three days before the wedding my determination to respect her choice snapped. I worried all night, took a bus and turned up on her doorstep at seven o'clock in the morning. I told her the hell with the dress and the food and the invitations. If she didn't want to do this she didn't have to. She started to sob; then she told me she was pregnant. I gave up and we drank coffee together. I could see that she needed this one to have a father. At least I knew why she looked so sick.

It took twenty awful months but in the end she gathered up all three children and ran for it to a woman's refuge. The refuge has been closed down since then - not cost-effective, I presume. I hope to God there is still somewhere left for a woman to find safety from an abusive partner.

The day before I was due to defend my dissertation Bob died. Dear clever witty complicated Bob. I was offered a postponement but hadn't the sense to accept it. I don't think a more forceful defence would have made much difference; the examiners required the addition of explanatory sentences in the academic manner before they would accept it. (I took them all out again before it was published). Ten months later I was still trying to oblige them. Not as easy as you might think. For instance: 'If you have used a word which accurately expresses what you wish to convey do not subsequently attempt to find a different word in order to avoid repetition. Use the same word again.' The same word. It's against nature. When I find myself accidentally repeating one I have to decide which of them has the stronger claim; one of them has to go. But it's the academics' game. You have to play by their rules.

XXII

I was spending the evening with Tatisha when Emma phoned. She said 'There's no other way of telling you this. Matthew's dead'. She was fighting to get the words out and I loved her for being so direct. At 3 a.m. I identified Matthew in High Wycombe hospital. His twenty-eight-year-old wife Fiona and their two boys, William three and Tom one, had been having a brief break in a caravan in Devon and were on their way home. Matthew, who was thirty-eight, had died on a motorway in a motor-cycle accident. He was working as a courier. Not speeding (police evidence). Trying to avoid hitting the car whose driver had pulled out without looking. The man was fined £500 and lost a few points on his licence. Did they not understand? This was my son.

Waking up was the worst. The momentary joy of discovering that it was just another nightmare and the immediate realisation that it was not. You'll be glad to hear that I'm not going to tell you how I felt. The poems I started writing a year later, on the train, returning home from the crematorium on the first anniversary of his death, are there at the end of the book. It had taken me a year to understand that this problem, unlike a lot of other problems, has only one solution. I wrote those first four lines on the back of an envelope. The rest followed.

By this time Eileen had long since decided that she could no longer care for Neil. He was in hospital at the time, recovering from a minor operation, and was discharged to a local home for the elderly. He was desperate. Jenny Fernald had spoken of Denville Hall as a splendid retirement home for actors run by the Royal Theatrical Fund; the children and I decided to see if they would accept a stage-designer. Warren Mitchell, good friend and lovely actor, spoke for him as having had a very successful, if brief, career in the theatre, and I sat with Neil while the two of us compiled a list of all the productions he had designed. He spent the last years of his life in a home run as all such homes should be run. Like a really good hotel with excellent food and a bar and medical care instantly available. He had quite forgotten that we were divorced; when I visited him he always introduced me as his wife, a position which was easy to resume as I'd never felt like anything else.

Now I went to Denville Hall to tell him about Matthew. I found him apparently unmoved although a nurse had already broken the news to him. He asked if I would take him to see Matthew's body. I phoned the Maudsley for advice; they thought that he might come to regret that he had not seen his son that one last time. So I booked a car and went with him to the funeral directors. He walked into the room where Matthew lay and tried to hang his stick on a handle of the coffin. When it wouldn't fit he turned away and propped it up in the corner. Then he took a look, picked up his stick and walked out. He was perfectly calm; I was on the edge. I asked if I could move the cloth that covered Matthew's body I wanted to see his hand. Well, I wanted to hold it and kiss it actually. 'It's very dirty' the man said. He's not a tramp, he's a biker, I longed to shout. I went back into the room alone and kissed his grimy biker's hand, trying to ignore the tasteful frizz of artificial hair that covered one side of his head.

Neil didn't speak on the way back to Denville Hall. I thought perhaps the presence of the driver was making it hard for him. I waited until we were alone in his room with cups of tea and said 'Now we can talk.' He smiled a knowing smile. 'Do you remember Madame Tussauds?' he asked me. And that was the position he maintained till the end of his life. This was one loss too many. What he had seen was not Matthew. It was a wax-work.

He came to the funeral with a nurse from Denville Hall, sat at the back of the crematorium in his wheel-chair and left before the wake. Lucy saw him sitting in the car and ran to say goodbye. He opened the window and gave her the same knowing smile. Then wagged his finger at her. It was easier for Neil to believe that we had all played this hideous practical joke on him than to believe in Matthew's death. He had retreated into his psychotic bolt-hole and unhappened another bad thing. For a moment I envied him.

Every year or so I tried to approach the subject but his only response was the smile. We never spoke about Matthew again.

A PhD. seemed an irrelevance. I stopped writing. Then, some months after Matthew's death I received a phone-call. Rimas Tumenas was bringing The Little Theatre of Vilnius to this country with his production of Lermontov's 'Masquerade'. He wanted a translation from the Russian original to use as surtitles. Jane, the Dr. Grayson who had introduced me to Bulgakov at SSEES, suggested me. The representative of the company phoned me. I refused. She persevered. I said I'd try. There was no time for a verse translation; I did a prose version and accompanied them to Belfast for the opening night. Then I came back and set about finishing the PhD. I was functioning, but changed.

XXIII

I didn't go to Moscow in the following winter. I may have been to Paris. Yes. Paris was in 2000. I had been awarded the Pushkin gold medal for translation in 1999, the bicentenary of his birth, by the Association of Creative Unions in Moscow, and the presentation was to take place at the Russian Mission to UNESCO. God I was lonely. No one was free to come with me – my eight grandchildren's ages now ranged from two to eleven, no one had any money and I stayed for two days because the ticket on Eurostar was cheaper than staying for one. Every time I opened my mouth, I found that my schoolgirl French had been replaced by Russian. The Mission's hotel for visitors was a welcome refuge. Still Soviet-brown but welcoming. I did venture out to see the Eiffel Tower, as it was said to be nearby. Inevitably I got lost, constructed a question and looked about me for a friendly face. The woman I eventually chose said 'I'm sorry, I don't speak French'. In Russian. It was a joyous moment. That medal is precious to me. In the event of a fire I would grab it. But I was glad to be back in London again.

At this point I really took my eye off the ball. The publishers of my dissertation said they would like to have something else of mine. I suggested Griboedov's letters and signed the contract. Finish your greens before you have any pudding. Don't misunderstand me. His letters are revealing, witty, informative – but they are written, understandably, in prose. And it is poetry I love to translate. Pushkin's poetry. To compound the felony, I decided to learn ancient Greek, in order to read the Meditations of Marcus Aurelius in the original. The Roman's preference for Greek as the language of the upper classes seems so like the Russian addiction to French of Pushkin's generation. 'The only civilised language ....'. Pushkin put a stop to all that by writing in Russian. Well. I suppose Napoleon helped. Why Marcus Aurelius? Claire, my Tuesday-evening flautist, had given me a translation of it just when I needed it. Do read him if you haven't. He is so full of human uncertainty, clearly anxious about death. 'Wait in peace for extinction', he tells himself. Then adds, clinging to hope, 'or an altered state'. I've argued with him in the margins but I never did read him in Greek. I got side-tracked by Plato. Or Socrates ... I shall never regret reading the 'Phaedo'.

About six years later when I'd just finished reading some dialogues of which the 'Phaedo' was one, it came to me. 'Are you insane? What do you really want to do? You are 80. Were you planning to live for ever?' I abandoned Greek and wrote to the publishers asking to be released from my contract. I'd finished translating the Griboedov letters but the task of checking the spelling of every village in the middle-east, some long-since re-named, which Griboedov had visited and transliterated, would have taken me more time than I was prepared to give it. I knew perfectly well what I really wanted to do. I wanted to finish my verse translation of Pushkin's great novel in verse. I got up next morning at 6 a.m. as usual, took my usual tray of tea and an apple back to bed and opened 'Evgenii Onegin'. I felt like the prodigal son. I'd come home.

Life had been going on during those six years; days got longer, years got shorter. My ability to remember the sequence of things is definitely declining; the things themselves remain vivid. My PhD. ceremony – worth it for the hat. I love hats, and this one was so beautiful; wide, flat, black-velvet, with a crimson tassel that hung down on one side. Worn with a crimson robe, its hood and folds edged with blue. What's not to like? as my children would say. I continued to spend part of every winter in Moscow; with one exception it is where my Russian friends are. Let me tell you about the exception. Do you remember Irina? with whom I shared a room at the Pushkin Institute? We lost touch after I went home in 1991. It must have been ten years later when I answered the phone in Catford and a Russian woman told me that she had a letter for me from Irina; the following winter I flew from Moscow to Irkutsk.

The time I have spent in Russia comes to me in disconnected memories of occasions which – I can hardly bear to acknowledge – cannot now be repeated. I know that I visited Irina twice more after that time in 2001, but the memories of Irkutsk appear in random scenes. The party when we met for the first time in ten years; the countryside in winter when we went to see her sister Liuba and her family; the bania-for-two in their garden and the serious steaming-ritual presided over by Liuba's friend, known as the 'iron lady' – 'zheleznaia ledi' – out of respect for Margaret Thatcher. Irina and I steamed together. The Iron Lady took her turn alone. Moans of extreme enjoyment were heard. Then a rhyming couplet which I've translated as: 'Aaagh that's good. That's good as sin. Send another soldier in.' The temperature was so high that the resin seeped out of the two wooden benches and stuck to the back of your legs; then kneeling in the snow – rolling would surely have been unseemly at my age – rubbing handfuls of it all over myself. (I didn't even feel cold). Lake Baikal, frozen at -40 degrees, warming our fingers eating hot fish that had been caught through ice-holes and roasted at the side of the lake; young men reading their poems at the Literary Institute; young teenagers turning out to read theirs although the schools were closed (they do at below -30 degrees, I think) at one of the Decembrist's houses, now museums.

Oh, and the interview. It took place in Liuba's kitchen. I sat at the table with her black cat on my lap making pelmeny. The cat was there by choice - have you ever tried to make a cat do anything? The pelmeny are like crescent shaped ravioli stuffed with minced beef, pork and onions, which Irina had already prepared. Alll I had to do was to stamp out little circles of pasta, fill them, bend them over into half-moons and bring the ends together while being interviewed and filmed by the television crew who had somehow managed to cram themselves and their equipment into that tiny room.

The interviewer asked me about translating Pushkin's poetry. How did it sound in English? I thought of the 'Tale of the Priest and his man Balda'. Very funny, calculated to annoy a lot of people, specially the church; a stupid grasping country priest gets his comeuppance from Balda, village idiot-come-hero. I recited the first few rambling couplets in Russian, then in English. Next morning Irina and I went shopping in the local market. As I paused to look at the fur hats the stall-holder said 'I know you. You're that woman who translated Balda'.

Balda might have been a mutual friend. One we both loved. Try asking a local stall-holder if they saw that Russian woman on telly last night talking about translating Byron.

I do love England too you know. Not just the beautiful bits, though there are plenty of those; not just some noble version of a past, lost and regretted. I love it here and now. Lively crowded Catford, where I am sometimes the only white person on the bus, where the stall-holders sell vegetables I wouldn't know how to cook and speak languages I don't understand. 'The universe is change...' (I know I've quoted that already and Catford is hardly the universe but I feel that Marcus Aurelius was having a really good day when he came up with that one.)

I had stayed several times with Dafydd, my good friend ever since we sat on the suitcases and talked about Russian literature; I had stayed with Lena, with Irina, with Svetlana ... Good friends all. But I lived with Marina; year after year after year. She had moved out of her own flat to make room for her daughter Masha, Masha's husband Igor and the two children, Fedia and Lisa. And to find room for her Shakespeare research. She shared her brother's flat until he moved permanently to Zaraisk. (I'll tell you about Zaraisk). Marina knows who wrote Shakespeare; it was Roger Manners, 5th Earl of Rutland, and who am I to argue? To say that as long as we have the words in that order feels like treachery. And she has very convincing arguments with which a lot of more knowledgeable people than I agree. Sasha, Marina's husband, is a constant support in their separate loving relationship.

This has been my home in Moscow. These people are my family in this other place where I live. Sasha or Masha always met me at the airport; if both their cars broke down they phoned a friend. Marina did once stay with me in Catford until her health made travelling more difficult. The New British Library was for her a Paradise; as long as it remained open she was there. Now she supervises her post-graduate translation students in her kitchen – a different kitchen, of course, but happily indistinguishable from the one where we first worked together on the 'Firebird'. The same tottering piles of books, files and papers on every flat surface. While her bedroom, where she sits at her computer, is the Bermuda triangle of important documents. Do not put one down in there. Not even momentarily. I'm telling you this because I know Marina will read my book and I know she won't mind. She has even offered to translate it.

Zaraisk is the other place where Marina lives when she's not working as a professor of translation; a small ancient town, about three hours from Moscow by car in a south-easterly direction. When the Mongols arrived in the 13th century they killed the local prince. His lady took her little son, climbed the high tower of the Kremlin and threw herself and her child to their deaths. The town's old name – something like Zarazesk – means 'the fall'. There is a surprisingly modern piece of sculpture commemorating this noble tragedy in the town, which now has a lively market and some light industry.

All this has nothing to do with me and Marina. We live at 42, Freedom Street, walking distance through fields to the river in which, two years ago, I swam. There the roads are lined with weeping birches and disintegrate at the edges into flowers, both wild and cultivated, and piles of useful things for building or burning. This is where the stand-pipes are – not everyone has water actually in the house. We do. Only cold when I first went there; now luxurious – and expensive – hot water which feeds a shower, though not the kitchen.

Zaraisk is a quiet place. I heard a cock crow there for the first time. If you see two cars at once it's the rush-hour. Our house is like so many others; a sort of log cabin with fascia boarding whose blue and green paint has faded to merge with the wild profusion of raspberries and nettles and pot-herbs and spring onions and hops which look as though they may be planning a takeover. The wooden window-frames are topped by patterned triangles, the roof is of corrugated iron and the ceilings are so low that I can change a light-bulb without standing on tiptoe. The house is lower than the apple tree which was probably planted when it was built; in summer its apples fall like thunder on the iron roof – I thought it was thunder when I first heard them.

This is a place where you can write. There is absolutely nothing else to do. I translated all the quotations from Russian poets other than Griboedov in my dissertation one winter. That was the year when we arrived to discover that the electricity had been turned off. Sasha offered to drive us back to Moscow – but they'd probably turn it on in a day or two, we thought. So we stayed. Marina and I sat at our separate tables under the two windows of her bedroom, she with her powerless computer and I with my smug fountain pen. We worked in silence until the light went, then sat at the table by the window in the next room, eating and drinking and talking. This has to be one of the greatest pleasures in life. The Russians have a word for it. 'Sumernichat.' To talk in the twilight. By candle-light in our case. Though the light of a full moon on deep untouched snow poured in at the window and eclipsed the candle.

Marina's house is a 'semi-detached bungalow'. Oh how that does not describe it. The other half belongs to yet another heroic babushka, Katia. She supported her whole family of alcoholics by making and selling home-brew; her husband, her son, his wife who hanged herself in an alcoholic moment; she brought up their two children, a boy and a girl. I worried for her. 'What if the police find out?' I asked. 'Oh they know', Marina said. 'But what can she do?' Generations of luke-warm sherry at Christmas seeped, unnoticed, from my thinking. I imagined the police station, stacked with the stuff.

Katia herself is very disapproving of alcoholics; on a walk through our village she pointed out each house where one or more of them lived. There were rather a lot of them, I admit. I suppose that would be the other thing you could do in Zaraisk. I still remember our first conversation. I struggled for a bit while she watched me patiently. Then she asked 'Are those teeth yours?' 'Some of them', I said. 'Well. Not many'. We laughed and I loved her for finding the common ground I couldn't. When Marina had cold water piped into the house she included Katia's half; Katia comes in and washes up after supper and brings us mushrooms if she's picked any. I still feel slightly guilty if she catches me drinking one small vodka.

Enough. For you, I mean – not for me. I could never have enough of Zaraisk. Guess what my friends at 52, Freedom St. gave me on my 85th birthday – a beautifully bound 3 volume edition of Pushkin. The complete works. Ha. You didn't expect that. One more thing. This really will be the last. It's about wasps.

Marina has a reverence for life worthy of Albert Schweitzer. On my first summer morning there, sitting at breakfast, I waved away a wasp. 'Don't do that', she said. 'They won't hurt you if you don't wave your arms about'. She put some honey on the lid of the closed jar, mixed in some water with her finger so that they wouldn't get their feet stuck, and invited them to join us. 'Bicarb for bees, winegar for wasps' I was thinking, looking about for some. Still – as there was no choice.

I have to tell you that I grew to love those wasps. I was always the first at the breakfast table. I spread the lid with honey, mixed in the water with my finger while the wasps crowded on to it, waiting for me to finish. One morning I found an open jam-jar on the table with a dead wasp in the small amount of remaining jam. I fished it out with a knife and it moved. It was alive. Just. But its wings were stuck to its sides as though it were lying to attention. I eased it off the knife onto a clean plate and gave it a careful shower with a teaspoonful of luke-warm water, then put it on the sill of the open window to dry out. I had forgotten the cats (three resident, two day-care). The wasp was still soggy when one of them jumped in at the window. Fear must have given it strength; it flew out into the sunshine. I don't know how long wasps live; I hope it's still breakfasting with Marina. She was right, you know. Not one sting, ever. All summer.

I do love Moscow as well. They say it has changed since the fall of the Soviets but I'm not so sure. I think it may just have reverted to what it was before they got their grey hands round its throat and closed all the places where people might have met to plan revolt. Or, in my case, to sit down. In 1990 there was nowhere to sit down. A person without a sense of direction always walks twice as far as anyone else and I used to long for a warm place with chairs and tea. Muscovites had their kitchens; I would go down into the nearest metro. Warm, with benches but no tea.

Now expensive cafés and restaurants fight it out in the centre. Brightly lit shops, boutiques, advertisements in flickering lights, so many cars that the movement of traffic is categorised like a storm, Force 9 being dead-slow or stop; everything is available – at a price. The only 'defitsit' is money (this used to be a joke). The divided society in action; stretch limos for the wealthy and little old ladies begging in the streets. It seems very much like the Moscow that Pushkin so disliked. I too have heard about what goes on in higher circles than mine, in case you were beginning to wonder, outrageous stuff which the majority of Russians seem powerless to influence: with rare exceptions they carve out a life for themselves, living alongside, but not with, whoever has power; serf-owning aristocrats or Porsche-owning oligarchs.

Once – only once – I saw two dead bodies in the street. Walking where, in those early days, I had been warned not to walk. Two men, lying face down on the pavement beside a wrecked car, their hands wired together behind their backs. A lower class of villainy altogether. The road was unusually quiet. Not a soul about. Or so I hoped when I saw the bodies. Just in case I decided to walk past, not changing pace, as though I hadn't noticed anything. I made it round the first corner and then ran for it, feeling like Mole, who would venture into the Wild Wood in spite of Ratty's warnings.

St. Petersburg was for the intellectuals. Perhaps it still is. Peter the Great had wanted to 'break a window into Europe' with his beautiful city – he was too successful for my taste. I love the extremes in Moscow, the sudden surprises; walk round the corner of a soaring concrete office block and you may find a little church with onion domes painted blue with gold stars. And anyway. I don't go to Moscow for the architecture – or the politics; I go to see my friends.

XXIV

A t first I only went to Russia in winter. Every December pensioners receive a 'cold-weather allowance' and I enjoyed mine in Moscow. It seemed an entirely appropriate use of it. Besides, it was the only way in which I could get to see my friends. If you have followed me this far you will have noticed my near-complete failure to earn any money. I did once translate a catalogue for a Diaghilev exhibition at the Barbican and something on archaeology for the British Museum, but that's about it. I have always worked. But money never seemed to enter into it. My numerous translations for the 'Complete Works of Pushkin in English', for instance. A most laudable enterprise, celebrating the bicentenary of his birth, with a Russian, American and English committee in Moscow. I had just completed my doctoral thesis when I was asked if I would undertake some narrative poems for it – no fee involved. Of course I agreed. A parody of 'The Rape of Lucrece' with the husband not at war but out hunting; fairy-tales in rhyming couplets or an old Russian story-telling language with neither rhyme nor metre which is also poetry; so many things I might never have read without the organisational genius of Iain Sproat, who cajoled and flattered and sent out photo-copies of the next task to the numerous translators and made it happen. That project had been argued over for at least ten years before he took it over.

I had been translating and re-translating the last six lines of Onegin for years, on the grounds that if I couldn't convey all their beautiful directness there really was no point in translating the rest. I couldn't, of course. You never can. But by the time I'd translated the rest of the novel I'd grown accustomed to this sad truth. Finally I joined up with those six lines. I wrote them out one last time and pressed my pen down on the final full-stop. There was a brief moment of exhilaration; it was like the meeting of the two teams constructing the Semplon Tunnel. Then I was overcome by a feeling of utter desolation. I had lived with Onegin and Tatiana for nearly eight years and now the party was over. I felt bereft. Close to tears. I rang Alicia, my first editor at Heinemann, extraordinary friend and poet, already terminally ill; within a couple of hours her yellow roses arrived. It was the response I needed and she understood it – now I was free to mourn. After a while I thought: 'I've finished a translation. Pushkin had finished a masterpiece. How did he feel?' I know what he is reputed to have said on completing it. 'Ay, you Pushkin, ay, you son-of-a-bitch'. But after that moment of triumph, that suddenly knowing the only way to finish it? I wrote my poem. Then I went looking for his. There had to be one. And there was. Eight lines written shortly after finishing his novel in verse on 25th September, 1830.

Here are the first two:

'This is the moment I craved; the work of long years is completed.

Why this mysterious unease, incomprehensible grief?'

I admit to punching the air and shouting 'Yes!' If I didn't live alone they would probably put me away.

That was the beginning of another book: ' After Onegin: the last seven years'. Pushkin was 31 when he finished 'Onegin'. He died at 38, defending his wife's doubtful honour in a duel. He only had seven years left. Marrying was his first, fatal move; what then? I started to translate again; not the great historical, political works like 'Boris Godunov' or 'The Bronze Horseman', the product of those years. I looked for the personal poems, the nostalgic re-visiting of fairy-tales his nanny had told him, heart-breaking lyrics, revealing bits of letters; not separated into their various genres but all jumbled together in exact chronological order. As he lived them. I wanted to make the diary of a state of mind.

There is so much I long to tell you about my late love-affair with Russia. Don't worry. I won't. I'll try to concentrate on these past few years. They started quietly enough with my usual winter visit in 2011. I needed the Moscow frost. Lying in bed on a morning in late January and hearing that most comforting of sounds – the 'skreep, skreep' of pavements being cleared of ice and compacted snow. Like being in a pram. You are warm and other people are taking care of you. A moment of total unreality.

I had havered over this visit. Neil, who had been cared for so well at Denville Hall, had aged prematurely, as his surgeon predicted. He could no longer stand, his speech had nearly gone, his general health had deteriorated. He had been so ill for so long on such a cocktail of anti-convulsant drugs over the years that his survival, at seventy-eight, was a cause for wonder. Should I risk leaving the country? Another crisis occurred almost as soon as I arrived in Marina's kitchen. I made plans to return at once and he recovered. But something had changed in him. His jealousy of his children had never allowed him to enjoy their success. When I took him the first disk that Emma made, singing her own songs, accompanying herself on the piano, he wouldn't hear it. At last, the jealousy had left him. She had brought him a good keyboard in the hope that he would use it to improvise again. He hardly touched it. Now he wanted her to sing and play to him. 'Who is this man?' she asked me. 'I've never met him'. (Callous humour, once acquired, is for life). She hadn't met him – but I had. Nearly sixty years ago. And the song that he most wanted to hear? ''swonderful, 'smarvellous, that you should care for me'. He died less than two months later.

Do you remember the poet from Kazakhstan whose work I translated in 1990 and whom I never met? Sixteen or seventeen years later she phoned me in Catford. She had read an article about me, tried the Russian Union of Translators and Lenia had put her in touch with Marina. Umut Kemelbekova, now president of the New Millennium Foundation, an organisation which promotes the appreciation of Russian language and its literature abroad. She wanted to make a short film about me. In 2009 the foundation published two little books, both with parallel texts; her poems with my translations and my poems for Matthew, translated by her husband Jan, poet and philosopher. I hung on just long enough to complete the final proof-reading with him; then sobbed uncontrollably while Umut hugged me. That's something I've only done twice. Once with Umut from Kazakhstan and once with my good friend Liuba from the Ukraine. Don't you sometimes wish the British would let go?

I have spent so many good evenings laughing and talking and eating and drinking with Umut and Jan and their friends. If I can persuade her Umut will sing her country's folk-songs in a voice which at first sounded harsh to my western ears and is utterly beguiling.

They - the foundation, really, but I think of it as 'they' - Umut (her name means hope) the powerful driving force, Jan quietly chairing the advisory committee - they awarded me their prize for foreign translators of Russian literature. And a lovely thing has arisen from their annual poetry competition for school-children. I thought that if my publications in Russia ever earned enough roubles to buy a book I'd like to join in by presenting it to the winning poet. Umut had a better idea. The publication of the young person's work as the Mary Hobson prize 'so that her name will remain in Russia'. I have the first book of poems and short stories by a very talented sixth-former. I translated the first poem for it. Now that I can't be there myself it makes me so happy.

Latterly I had been visiting Russia in summer as well, sometimes to speak at a conference but mostly because that's when Marina goes to Zaraisk. I went to Moscow twice in 2011, the second time on the fourth of June.

'Kanal Kultura is interviewing you here tomorrow for the Pushkin programme on the sixth' Marina said as soon as I arrived. (Kanal Kultura is what it sounds like – an excellent T.V. programme of wall-to-wall culture). 'Then on July thirteenth you're going to Astrakhan to speak at a conference'. No one had mentioned Astrakhan. 'Won't it be hot?' I asked her. It would be hot. I turned my attention to the interview. I speak almost no Russian in London; it usually takes me two or three days to get my ear in. This time I would have to get my ear in by tomorrow morning. (I do get interviewed from time to time in Russia, owing to the happy fact that Russians take poetry seriously, even when translated).

Marina and I watched the programme with Kristina, our Finnish neighbour who lives just down the corridor. And here's the best bit. I had told the young woman who interviewed me that the last six lines of 'Onegin' were, for me, among the most beautiful he ever wrote, and that I could not remember them without emotion. Recklessly, I spoke them, the lines for which I had spent years trying to find some adequate equivalent. They kept it in. They let me says those words, in Russian, to a Russian audience. On Pushkin's birthday.

Sobering up, I was glad that they mentioned the book-launch that evening. We had a good audience, quite a few of whom were unknown to me. People spoke. Ira (Moscow Irina) read Tatiana's last six stanzas, her final words to Onegin, and I read my translation of them. Then I spoke for a bit and a friendly discussion ensued. I felt that I had spent the whole day, from morning to evening, in the company of people who love what I love. It's a rare pleasure.

Astrakhan is where the Volga finally reaches the Caspian Sea – you probably knew that, but I didn't. We travelled there by train on July 13th in air-conditioned comfort for 32 hours. Starched sheets, constant supply of boiling water for tea or coffee at the end of the corridor and – best of all – good company. Lënia, Leonid Gurevich, president of the Union of Translators of Russia, his wife Ania and a colleague of theirs, another woman translator. Various universities host this annual meeting and if I am unable to give you precise details of its purpose, apart from having a good time and laughing a lot, it is because when I stepped from the train onto the shadeless concrete platform the heat hit me. It was, I discovered later, even hot for Astrakhan; they were having a bit of a heat wave. I stood there in my hat and my factor 50 and thought 'Here I shall die'. I was 85 at the time and it seemed possible if not actually desirable.

I am ashamed – genuinely ashamed – to say that I failed to attend rather a lot of the conference. I spent whole mornings in my air-conditioned hotel room overlooking the Volga translating Pushkin's 'Golden Cockerel', one of his magical fairy-tales; Umut is publishing them all in Moscow soon, with pictures. I mean. I wasn't just lying about. On the day when the temperature reached 50 degrees and opening the door to leave the hotel was like opening the oven, we were taken on a guided tour of interesting places. On foot. Ania and I started by clinging to the strip of shade on the inner side of the pavement and trying to pay attention to our knowledgeable young guide. Then we gave up and made for any shade. My ignorance of Astrakhan remains untouched. I seem to remember a large white building; it may have been a cathedral. I would love to go back. In the autumn, perhaps. Or the winter.

We returned to the hotel and ate a hearty meal of meatballs and pasta. That gave me fifteen minutes before my taxi arrived to take me to the university where, it said on the programme, I was to deliver an 'Evening with Pushkin'. I peeled off my dress, showered, put on another one and ran for the lift. I have pictures of the occasion. Lenia on my right doing the introduction, a young woman student who was to read the bits of original Pushkin I needed on my left; and me in the middle, shining with sweat. Ah, but it was a wonderful evening. The audience was so welcoming and so ready to listen, the subsequent discussions so warm and full of laughter. I remember, there were flowers. And three students, who were too young to have grown up in the Soviet Union and had probably learned less poetry than their parents, told me 'You've made us fall in love with Pushkin all over again'. Bingo! Apples and pears rolling, money pouring from the fruit machine! I was so happy. Of course, there were only three of them. But you have to start somewhere. Now for the British.

As I near the end of my story and come closer and closer to the present, my memory is less secure; it's not the events I forget but their sequence. (I've already said that. You see?). I am told that this is a common symptom of old age, which is no help at all. Can 2011 really have been the year I went not only to Astrakhan and Zaraisk but to Irina and Vania's dacha? And then to Iasnaia Poliana, where Tolstoy lived and wrote 'War and Peace'? That would bring my Russian adventure to a most satisfying conclusion. And it did. Life is not usally so neat.

Irina and Vania are poets, translators, journalists, and Irina has translated many of my poems both beautifully and faithfully – you don't often get both. Little more than ten years ago they built themselves a dacha; respecting the ancient tradition, it is made entirely of wood and the bathroom is at the end of the garden. There is a comfortable contemporary shower and a high-tech flushing lavatory when you get there, but my Catford soul is addicted to convenience ... I spent such a friendly time there. We swam nearly every day. Once in a river whose name I've forgotten and then in what they called 'the pond', which gives no sense of its size. Irina's parents live in the neighbouring dacha; her mother and I played table-tennis in their garden and I tried to recall North Camp and Brian's lessons. I told her about Brian, and when occasionally I managed to put an evil spin on the ball she would shout 'Ha! Po-soldatski!'

The dacha was near Tula, home of the best spice-cakes ever and the eminent academic Iurii Lotman, whose obituary I translated to buy Matthew and Fiona a wedding present. It was also near Iasnaia Poliana, to which they took me at the end of my stay, for the annual translator's conference, where I spoke on Griboedov's 'Woe from Wit' and presented a copy of my newly-published 'Onegin'. Five whole days living where Tolstoy lived and wrote. He is buried in that 'bright glade', not a strictly accurate translation of 'Iasnaia Poliana' but the way I think of it. No iron railings, no fence, no monument, not a stone; a grassy mound finally satisfies his life-long yearning for an unattainable simplicity. I had the pleasure of telling his grandson – surely I mean great-great-grandson? – that I had only started to study Russian because I read 'War and Peace'.

I remember the last evening of our stay there. The party at the little restaurant opposite the gates to the estate. Long tables on three sides of the room, spread with zakuski, that inevitable and irresistible first course of so many delicious things that you cease to worry about leaving room for the second. There was vodka of course, wine and – necessary accompaniment to any such gathering – singing. With so many different nationalities present, Turkish, Chinese, Dutch, Italian, it was decided that we should each sing one of our national songs. Oh God. It's happened to me before. Why do I always forget? All I could think of was Greensleeves, which reminded me of ice-cream vans. Then I thought of Millie's story about her mother, 'one of three beautiful sisters who came from Ireland', and had a go at Molly Malone (In Dublin's fair city?). I might have Irish blood in me. I do hope so. Cathy joined me – Cathy Porter, the only other English person there, translator of Tolstoy's wife's diaries, and we managed a whole verse together right to the last 'Alive, alive-o'.

I shall tell you one last thing and then call it a day. It took place in the February of the following year, 2012. Ira, who can recite the whole of 'Onegin' from memory – no, by heart, a dated expression but one closer to the truth of the matter – had read my translation of it with her sixth-form pupils; they decided to give me a present. Ira devised an evening at the little Pushkin museum on the Arbat, where he took his young wife Natalia after their wedding. Three Onegins and three Tatianas plus a supporting cast, speaking Pushkin's Russian and my English, performed the romantic aspect of Onegin. They sang, they played, they danced; I was invited to waltz with a young Pushkin in a curly black wig, tried a few steps and retired, defeated. It didn't matter. Afterwards I spoke a bit, thanked them all, read some excerpts of my work and signed a heap of my Onegins for all the participants. After which I was given a personal guided tour of the museum by the curator. Was I tired? she asked. Tired does not describe it. But I was, by then, in that reckless state of overdrive when anything is possible. I am so glad I didn't miss it. I saw everything in the company of a woman who evidently shared my feeling for Pushkin and knew everything I wanted to know. I laid the yellow roses I had been given at the foot of his tall desk where he stood to write and went home to a vodka. Possibly two.

That was to be my last time in Moscow. I am so glad I didn't know. Later that year I had a mini-stroke which put an end to further travelling. I had spent the whole morning trying and failing to turn my 'Onegin' into a compressed zipped file and email it to my publisher in London – failing in spite of Lucy's patient instructions, over the phone, step by step. Now I was getting ready to leave for a rehearsal at Calder's bookshop in The Cut; Peter Marinker had arranged a performance of a dialogue between Onegin and Tatiana from my translation and I was to do a short introduction. The phone rang. It was Emma. 'You just caught me' I said. 'I'm going to Waterloo for the rehearsal.' 'Mum. You're not going anywhere. Stay right where you are. I'm sending an ambulance. I'm coming.' Feeling odder by the minute I went to put both front doors on the latch and let my inner front-door slam. I had locked myself out. I went carefully down the iron fire-escape to Marion on the ground floor who has my keys. I seemed to be thinking but it was difficult to explain anything. Neither Emma nor Marion needed an explanation. She took me back to my flat and stayed with me until Emma and the ambulance arrived. By which time I was speaking slowly, sometimes, apparently, in Russian. Emma told them that slow was not usual. Not me at all, in fact. So they took me to a hyper-acute stroke unit. By the time my speech went completely I was already being examined by a doctor. As a consequence of which I was fluent again in a couple of days, well enough to go home. The National Health Service is the mark of a civilised society. Look after it, all you children out there. 'Grapple it to thy soul with hoops of steel.' Or you'll lose it.

I have enjoyed being old. I intend to go on doing so. But there's a last time for everything. I tell myself that I shall stop writing after this before standards start to slip. Perhaps they already have and I don't know. And perhaps even that won't stop me. There is something so necessary about the quiet scratch of pen on paper, black ink meaning something. Now, at 87, I look at the confident young with love and admiration. When I started to write this autobiography I was constantly stopped in my tracks by two thoughts: 'Who on earth would want to know all this?' and 'Do I want them to?' What kept me at it was the belief that even now, among those uninhibited masses, there might still be someone waiting for life to start. If there is, and you happen to be reading this book, I want to tell you. You'll get there. You will. For us it just takes a little longer.

Death and the Biker

For Matthew

Here are the poems I promised you. I started writing them exactly a year after my son Matthew's death on March 30th 1999. I was in the train alone, returning from the crematorium. I had taken him white flowers he couldn't see or care about. Then at last it occurred to me. This problem has no solution. It is the chord that cries out – like me – for resolution. The perfect cadence. But the problem of loss has no resolution. I found an old envelope and a pen in my handbag and wrote those first four lines. I had never written poems before – well, two, when deeply depressed. Now more poems came, quickly at first, then more slowly, over the next few years. My lovely publisher in Russia, Umut Kemelbekova, produced a beautiful little book of them. I hugged her and wept with her over the proof reading. But I had made up my mind. I was going to live with his loss, to do more, not less, for as long as possible, and remember him.

London, 2014

Now I will always know that you died.
Now I am an imperfect cadence,
only to be resolved
by my own death.

March 2000

Movement of Trains

Thoughts,
like stones in a sieve,
jostle for survival.
Wheels clatter
over the rails.
Details
are shaken through the dusty grid,
witty unspoken retorts,
what they said, what he did,
leaving the ones that matter.
And you live
with your own,
travelling only to postpone
arrival.

They'll say 'Do you remember when..?'
We'll be together then.
Ah, that's a too late joy.
To be remembered with my boy.

Death and the Biker

I'd give my life to hear you
executing the Moonlight Sonata;
You as executioner,
Beethoven as martyr.
You loving the sense
of incongruity,
white music, black leather,
tongue tense,
a parody of assiduity,
holding your few bars together.

Sunday morning with Matthew and his boy

'You had this.'
He smiled, suddenly knowing
the common bliss
of a child, growing.

Waterloo Station

How can it be
That I am buying flowers for you?
It's not a thing that mothers do.
You should have chosen them for me.

The Counsellors

Who dares tell me how to grieve?
Who dares tell me what I should believe?
I will live with your death.
And I will live with your laughter
till my dying breath.
Who dares to say
that we shall meet one day
in some illusory hereafter?

Weather Forecast

The roads are dry today.
Good visibility.
No rain till later on, they say.
Next news at three.
Why do I listen when he isn't there?
Why do I care?
The forecast is a charm
to keep some other mother's son from harm.
I hope it may.
But it's too late for me.

Top-box

I kneel before the piles
of mottled grey box-files
and shuffle through the academic dross
to find some poem, half-translated.
It should be in the top box now,
I think. Oh, don't allow
those words to mean
the courier's load,

the biker on the road.
Don't let me hear 'A Birmingham on board,
wait and return.'
Don't let me see your smile
as you ride off to earn
Your seventy pence a mile.
I can't afford
to start again,
lock up the pain,
rebuild the walls around the ache,
remake
the boundaries of loss.

Sheep Pen

My thoughts break loose like stupid sheep.
I just can't keep
the woolly fools from doing harm.
They trample on the Astro Turf of calm
that I've laid down, obligatory balm
for those who need to think
I'm 'getting over it'. They sink
sharp hooves into the brightly covered ground
and only searching for the word will round
them up and write them back into the pound.

The Half-life

No bliss, no dread,
no plan ahead.
The half-life. A convenient way
to fill the day.
It's all that I can spare.
The rest is on the road
beside him there,
beside the spinning wheels, the scattered load.

Eclipse

It seems unreasonable to complain
that joy cannot be whole again.
I knew the risk.
I knew that it could suffer the eclipse
that marks each rounded moment with its dark elipse,
that shadows each bright disc.
I knew the risk –
but who could guess the pain?

Summer Wedding

The boy was bored. He found the swimming pool
behind the high hedge, green and cool.
The unaccustomed tie, the tight white shirt,
a crumpled eight of trousers hit the dirt
and, glorious in the sun, he floundered in,
the fierce cold puckering his grateful skin.
At three, champagne left luke-warm in the living room,
a garden group of guests posed with the bride and groom
(apart from one or two who slept).
Obedient to the call, the good child leapt
out of the pool and ran to join them there,

wet, naked, unaware.
The guests, all hatted, gloved and frocked,
were shocked.
They should have cheered – or so it seemed to me –
that joyous symbol of fertility.

I wish I could be sure you didn't know
you had to go and leave your boys.
I want to think that you went out
with one last angry shout
of 'Fuck!' One wrench, one swerve,
one blow, the twitch of one last nerve.
Then silence. Nothing. No more noise
of sirens, ambulances, no regret
for all the things you hadn't finished yet.
I wish I could be sure.
And still I doubt.

They cannot be the boys they would have been.
They may be kind and clever, brave and strong,
they may have every grace,
the ones who take their place,
but we have lost the boys he would have seen
grow into men. Can it be wrong
to mourn their loss with his?
What if it is.
They cannot be the boys for whom I long.

The one last thing

While I was living and complaining
it was going.
While I was making meals and sewing,
without my knowing,
or anyone explaining,
I had the best of it.
I didn't think that it would last for ever.
I'd heard of death.
Why did I waste the best of it?
Not taste the best of it?
While I had breath
I should have given them – oh, I don't know, but more,
my four.
Was I too stupid or too clever?
Oh let me try again.
I promise not to mind the pain.
You fool. Keep quiet and live the rest of it
as though you didn't mind.
Be old and kind.
Give them the one last thing.
Show them that death does ultimately lose its sting.

By Eurostar to Paris

I can be lonely anywhere.
Trains, parties, supermarkets – it's a gift.
I feel this rift.
There's me.
And then there's all humanity.
It isn't something you can say aloud,
but yes – I'm proud.
I've managed to avoid despair.

I try to understand
what people do
that gets them through the day,
and if they planned
to live that way.
My curiosity supplies
a momentary link to them.
Are they pretending
that there's a happy ending?
Or are they just heroic,
impenetrably stoic?
I peer through my disguise
and drink to them.

The pain's the same size as the love.
How can I wish it less?
The pair of them are hand in glove.
It's hard to guess
which one hurts most.
The hell with it. I'll play the host
to pain, I'll make a friend of it,
and wait for death to make an end of it.

I used to be afraid of death.
Oh happy, happy fear,
when I had everything to lose
and all my love was here.
I've only lost a part of it.
There's plenty more to take.
But I must part with all of it
before I lose this ache.

Our shared laughter
denied all rumours of a bright hereafter.
So we loved then, when it was now.
That's how,
right from the first,
I never knew the worst
regret. The one that plagues the lonely.
Between us there is no 'if only'...

Junk food

Sweet-sour pork, Hong-Kong style, couldn't kill you,
nor could Cadbury's cream eggs by the box.
When you lay there, so solid and still, you
were strong, they said. Strong as an ox.
That powerful heart should be beating.
Those great arms should be round your wife.
All that loving and laughing and eating
should be feeding your hunger for life.

'My life isn't big enough.' *Matthew, March 6th, 1966*

It was the night before your fifth birthday.
You came into the kitchen where
I laboured to display
my skill and make
a tipper-lorry out of cake.
What awful prescience made you say
those words. I didn't feel that I was being blamed
and yet I felt ashamed
to fuss about the birthday tea,
in face of your philosophy.

Death and the Biker

Ah, had you somehow guessed
that you must hurl yourself at life
and seize the best,
the biker friends, the rock and roll, your boys, your wife,
before death snatched the rest?
I didn't dare
to know what you had said.
I sent you back to bed.

Perhaps I've tried too hard
to hide my grief.
But I am always on my guard
lest I should undermine the widely-held belief
that I can be the same,
unchanged, undamaged by the blow.
Well – friends are not to blame.
I've played their comfortable game.
How could they know?

Everyone has very sensibly
decided to move on.
Except for me.
The gulf between us widens by the minute.
I see their future but I am not in it.
The past has gone
to parody itself in dreams.
That leaves the present.
A moving point of grief,
brief,
but doggedly reducing the extremes
of joy to pleasant.

Grapes and a Rolls-Royce

When you were three
you promised me
That you would give me grapes and a Rolls-Royce.
When you grew up, you said.
And when you did
you saw
that there were things I needed more
and gave them all with tireless generosity.
Now you are dead
I touch the shelves you made for me,
recall the cars you mended,
the jokes you shared, the pain you hid,
and know that in that childish choice
of grapes and a Rolls-Royce
lay something rare and splendid.

Well. There's another year
you didn't have. Another year in which
you didn't thunder up my iron stairs
to drink sweet tea
and tell me you were getting rich
and what you earned last week
in courier-speak –
'A Birmingham on board, wait and return.'
(You're paid both ways, you see.)
Now it's my turn
to visit you.
Bring you another of my atheist prayers
and then do what I always do.
Live through
another year still loving you.
It's why I'm here.

A Meditation on Marcus Aurelius

The actor who complained that he had not
spoken his five acts, only three.

'In life three acts are the whole play.
So leave the stage.
Be reconciled.'
I have to say,
my good friend from another age,
that here your excellent advice rings hollow.
That actor was my child,
and those were three hard acts to follow.

You know those little bits of food
that you save in the fridge
to throw away later?
And you know those trains
that are too long for the platform
so that the last doors don't open?
Well. Would you mind
if I didn't save myself
to go mouldy behind the last doors?

Earlsfield Station

I waited for the train.
The orange dots composed themselves
to deliver their halting message.
'Due to an earlier power...'
Ah, due to an earlier power
I loved,
had children,
made plans,
squandered time...
'failure' the dots continued,
but I had lost interest in their message.

I stood at the roadside
and waited for the green man
I didn't grudge the blind
their raised polka-dots,
but my feet were not happy.
And my carriers were

expecting to be carried.
A wrinkled black woman
looked at them critically.
'That's too much for you', she said.
She was right, of course.
But as usual,
I hadn't recognised unbearable
until I'd paid for it.

Grief-counsellors are all the rage.
They see bereavement as a three year trial.
Denial
is the initial stage;
then comes acceptance, anger, parting with the past,
until at last
you realise
that you are able to internalize
your feelings for the one you love
and, having worked your way through the above,
arrive at 'closure',
they tell you, with professional composure.
Are they insane?
Have they somehow avoided pain?
Or is their own loss so profound
that they prefer to sound
the depths of someone else's black despair
which, after all, is easier to bear.

March 8th 2003

I went to Scotti's Snack-Bar yesterday.
'Café Bastardo', as you used to say.
They still remember.
Your picture's propped up on the ledge.
You on your bike, while Adam reads the A to Z.
He's dead,
they say. A car crash. Last December.
The couriers have gone.
They've all moved on.
Antonio, Maria, Al and Max
serve snacks
to secretaries on a diet.
There's not much call for fry-ups now.
It's all gone quiet.
I sit there, on the edge,
and show the snaps. Maria tells me how
the boys are just like you.
'Is juss like Matthew. Jussa same.'
I hear her say.
I drink my tea.
Antonio won't let me pay.
Maria says 'I tellya what I do.
I put 'em in 'is picture. See?
Is jussa same.'
But Al says 'No. That's an unlucky frame.'

Insulation

You are wrong, John Donne.
I can't be the only one
to discover that, though I may long
to belong
to your interdependent communion of souls,

I have spent all my life building rickety boats
and I've never made something that floats
quite as far
as where they all are.
I'm an island. One. On my own.
And when the bell tolls
for me, as it will,
I shall still
be alone.

Laundry Blues

I sort all the dirty clothes night after night.
Delicate dark, delicate light,
tough dark, white wash, cold wash only,
separate piles. What it means to be lonely.
Pour in the powder and press the right switch.
Why do I care what's with what, which is which?
Would it be terrible, day after day,
to stuff them all in under 'delicate grey'?
To dance all night in the delicate dark,
greet the dawn in the delicate light of the park,
while the tough dark days are white-washed out
and the cold wash boils till its steam runs out?

The Spanish have a saying:
'Take what you want – and pay for it.'
I'm paying.
And yet.
If I had known the price
would I have hesitated?
No love, no loss, and life a well-hedged bet,

all risk eliminated?
I wouldn't have thought twice.
I took the best.
As for the rest,
safe is the best that you can say for it.

I can't help feeling sorry for
The ape who was the first to find
That he could look inside his mind
and, what was more,
in spite of all his unaccustomed mental labours,
he couldn't look inside his neighbours';
when, slowly, he deduced from this
that they could not look inside his.
That must have been the moment when,
alone,
with no way back
into the pack
of his once-fellow less-than-men,
the first of all mankind,
he lost his nerve, poor sod,
and, needing to be known,
invented God.

It isn't real, this peace that distance brings,
this knowing that you're gone
and getting on
with things.
I should have guessed.
Music went first.
I waited for the moment where
my hair
would stand on end. It wasn't there.
Nor was the thirst
for that one phrase my memory rehearsed.
It came at last – and passed to join the rest.
But I remained unblest.
I see what I have done
I see the cost of what I've won.
I've made this lousy deal.
The wound will seem to heal
as long as I don't feel.
Well come on Bach and Mozart, do your worst.
Come on Will Shakespeare, Pushkin, Austen, join the queue.
The deal is off. I've got to be
the me
you knew.

Four poems for Marina, with my love

Snow in Moscow

The snow has tidied the streets again.
It never learns.
We'll only trample it into mud,
shuffle it into the metro,
sweep it about in brown lakes.
Still. You have to admire
its beautiful persistence.

Snow in Zaraisk

A dangerous weight of snow
is overhanging my window.
It slid from the roof for a foot or two
one sunny morning.
But the frost caught it.
So there it hangs,
in suspended animation,
waiting for spring.
Embedded in the icy underside of this projection,
etched blackly, like a fly in white amber,
a twig with three berries
and a skeletal leaf,
trapped by the first snow,
waits with it.
I am keeping an eye on things.
Dripping, dependent icicles have appeared.
The fall will be spectacular.

Summer in Zaraisk or Who wrote Shakespeare?

Zaraisk is green.
I mean,

not just politically correct,
but green, unchecked,
in glorious profusion and neglect.
Here raspberries and nettles grow together,
and mischievous young devils
play out Shakespeare's midsummer revels
in summer weather.
Here Dima's sunflowers grow like weeds –
his parrot eats the seeds –
and here Marina reads
John Donne,
in search of further proof
that Rutland was the one,
and apples fall like thunder on the roof.

Another winter in Zaraisk...

At 42, on Freedom Street,
how shall I say – it's less than neat.
It wouldn't pass a test. But that's
because of three rambunctious cats.
What gives it dignity and status
is that it's home to two translators
who sit and read and write and then,
next day, go at it all again.

At 42, on Freedom Street,
Shakespeare and Pushkin, they compete.
It is the cultural centre of
Zaraisk, you know. Forget Tambov.
It's warm and welcoming and low,
besieged by scintillating snow.
New Russians would despair of it.
I wouldn't change a hair of it.

Translator's lament (To Umut and Ian)

On Saturday I wrote the last full-stop.
Onegin was to be
my swansong. Probably
the swans have better timing,
but I'm still here. Bereft. What's worse,
after this long apprenticeship in verse,
there's no escape.
I'm like an athlete over-running the tape,
I'll rhyme until I drop.
I am addicted to iambic rhyming.
While I could sit in bed
and English everything he said
and tear my brain apart
in an endeavour
somewhere between a crossword and fine art –
life was splendid.
And then it ended.
I wrote the final line.
I knew it couldn't last for ever,
But I was safer inside Pushkin's head.
It isn't half as comfortable in mine.

No need to argue, Mr Dawkins

It's clear that there is nothing to connect
religion with the intellect;
it's more a state of mind,
one common to brilliant persons and the less refined.
Your simple peasant faith will always be
a pure gold coin, a valid currency.
But turn it over and you'll see,
there on the back of it,
my simple peasant lack of it.

You've gone to ground
in some safe place you've found.
I do the things that people do,
I hope and hope and eat and drink
and think
that I'm not thinking about you.
But then I'm walking through a crowd
and suddenly I find I've said your name. Aloud.
And strangers stare to meet
another mad old lady on the street.

Despair

I hate this page.
No black on white,
no crossings out, not one scrawled word.
It is demanding that I write,
empty my head,
release my rage,
my love of the absurd,
my grief.
Well yes. It would be a relief.
Something I need to do.
A chore.
Like clearing dead leaves from the overflow.
But is it anything you'd like to know?
Why should I empty it on you?
It's all been said
before.

'But then begins a journey in my head',
Will Shakespeare said.
Ah, there's a man who knew
a thing or two;
whose unquiet spirit travelled through the night,
knowing the longed-for light
would bring him no respite.
I hadn't read that sonnet
for quite a while, and then I came upon it.
Mind you, no jewel hangs for me in ghastly night.
My black is black.
But all the same,
I recognize the game
we share,
the headful of despair,
so welcome back,
fellow insomniac.

Loss and the British

Why
do we try
to be so tough?
Why do we cling
to this unnatural obligation?
Would it outrage the nation
if
our upper lips were less than stiff?
Why don't we howl
throw in the towel,
give up, give in, admit we've had enough?
But no.
We plan the funeral, choose the music, organise.
No screams of pain, no cries.
Then, by the time we've done the decent thing
and crept back to what used to be
normality,
it is too late.
We are too distant from that first pure grief,
beyond belief
and inescapable.
The moment wouldn't wait.
And we are left,
bereft,
incapable
of telling all the things that we left unexpressed...
How can we think that this is 'for the best'?

CPSIA information can be obtained at www.ICGtesting.com
Printed in the USA
BVOW06s0836150416

444342BV00011B/106/P